DOCTOR WHO SPECIAL EFFECTS
M A   E

By arrangement   oration

Beaver Books

For Bernard and Ian

A Beaver Book

Published by Arrow Books Limited
62–5 Chandos Place, London WC2N 4NW
An imprint of Century Hutchinson Ltd

London Melbourne Sydney Auckland
Johannesburg and agencies throughout the world

First published 1986

Dr Who series © British Broadcasting Corporation 1986
Text © Mat Irvine 1986
Photographs © Mat Irvine 1986

This book is sold subject to the condition that
it shall not, by way of trade or otherwise, be lent,
resold, hired out, or otherwise circulated without the
publisher's prior consent in any form of binding or cover
other than that in which it is published and without a
similar condition including this condition being imposed
on the subsequent purchaser.

Book design Cherriwyn Magill
Cover design Andy Chappin

Set in 12 point Plantin

Made and printed in Great Britain
by Scotprint, Musselburgh, Scotland

ISBN 0 09 942630 7

CONTENTS

INTRODUCTION
5

1 SPECIAL EFFECTS IN THE BEGINNING
7

2 BEHIND THE SCENES ON 'DOCTOR WHO'
13

3 PLANNING EFFECTS
17

4 CONSTRUCTING EFFECTS
24

5 'DOCTOR WHO' AND THE TV STUDIO
31

6 ON LOCATION
37

7 MODELS AND MINIATURES
43

8 MONSTERS AND CREATURES
61

9 THE DALEKS
67

10 K-9 – THE DOG
72

11 THE TARDIS
81

12 'DOCTOR WHO' IN THE FUTURE
84

CHRONOLOGY
93

GLOSSARY
93

INDEX
95

ACKNOWLEDGEMENTS

THE MAJORITY OF the photographs used in this book were taken by the author but are the copyright of the BBC. The two exceptions are on p. 86 Quantel's Paintbox which is reproduced by kind permission of Quantel Ltd, and p. 91 the Imax screen reproduced by kind permission of the National Museum of Photography, Film and Television, Bradford.

The cover photograph is of a Silurian © BBC 1970.

The inside photographs are as follows: pp. 1 & 76 © BBC 1984; p. 6 (top) © BBC 1955; (bottom) 1984; p. 8 © BBC 1978; p. 10 © BBC 1975; p. 11 © BBC 1979; p. 12 (top left) © BBC 1980; (top right) © BBC 1977; (bottom left) © BBC 1981; (bottom right) © BBC 1975; p. 16 © BBC 1985; p. 18 © BBC 1981; p.21 © BBC 1985; p. 22 © BBC 1985; p. 25 © BBC 1978; p. 26 © BBC 1983; p. 27 (top left) © BBC 1981; (top right) © BBC 1981; p. 30 © BBC 1981; p. 33 © BBC 1978; p. 36 © BBC 1983; p. 39 © BBC 1981; p. 40 © 1978; p. 42 © BBC 1978; p. 45 (top) © BBC 1980, (bottom) © BBC 1981; p. 46 © BBC 1981; p. 47 © BBC 1981; p. 50 (top and bottom) © BBC 1981; pp. 54–5 © BBC 1980; pp. 58–9 © BBC 1981; p. 60 © BBC 1970; p. 62 © BBC 1977; p. 63 © BBC 1975; p. 65 © BBC 1973; p. 66 © BBC 1973; p. 68 © BBC 1966; p. 70 © BBC 1966; p. 71 © BBC 1984; p. 73 © BBC 1981; p. 76 (top) © BBC 1984; (bottom) © BBC 1981; p. 78 © BBC 1981; p. 79 © BBC 1977; p. 80 (above) © BBC 1983; (below far left) © BBC 1963; (below left) © BBC 1976; p. 85 © BBC 1978; p. 88 © BBC 1984; p. 92 © BBC 1977.

The author and publishers would also like to thank: Gundan Robot, p. 18; Tom Baker, pp. 18 and 25; R. J. Lehmann, p. 25; Lalla Ward, p. 30; David Weston, p. 30; Norman Comer and Vincent Brimble, p. 36; Ian Sears, Bill Fraser and Gillian Martell, p. 39; Gabriel Wolfe, p. 63; Jan Chappell and David Jackson, p. 85.

The author and publishers would also like to thank the following *Dr Who* writers: Bob Baker (K-9), Stephen Harris (Sutek and Hordas), Malcolm Hulke (Silurian), David Fisher (Ogri), Stephen Gallagher (Tharil, Privateer, Gundan robot), Dave Martin (K-9), Terry Nation (Daleks).

Every care has been taken by both the author and publishers to trace copyright holders. If we have inadvertently omitted to acknowledge anyone we should be most grateful if this could be brought to our attention for correction at the first opportunity.

INTRODUCTION

ONCE UPON A time I was part of a special effect myself – as the voice of K-9 on *Doctor Who* – so I suppose I must be uniquely qualified to write an introduction to this book!

Visual effects on film and television have always fascinated me, and from my ringside seat on *Doctor Who* and *Blake's 7* I learned quickly to appreciate the skill, imagination and sheer cunning of the technicians making them. (Mind you, I always used to stand well clear!)

Along with the Daleks, K-9 must rank as one of the best-known visual effects characters ever created on British television. Creating a personality for him was not too much of a hardship vocally, and he very soon joined the 'establishment' of science fiction cult figures. But where does technique end and mystique begin, I wonder? Mat was often called upon to drive K-9 around at fetes and charity functions when people would go up to him and say 'Go on, Mister, make him speak!', assuming that this effect could be produced at the flick of a switch. On the other hand, my actor friends would often rib me about 'having to get into that machine' every time I played K-9.

I am sure visual effects designers must be well used to the occasional technical hiccup, and I remember K-9's initial studio session was faintly alarming. For whenever he came in sight of the cameras, he would lurch around uncontrollably, bumping into the furniture, and the cameras would 'snow-up'. Apparently both were on the same radio frequency! There were other times (usually at some critical moment of filming) when K-9's drive belts or other vital organs would give away. Then Mat would have to bury his head in the 'works' and make urgent repairs – usually to the accompaniment of some pretty colourful language! Obviously there's far more to the world of visual effects than rummaging around in the entrails of a robot dog. I know you will enjoy the many other insights that Mat reveals in this book – without having to get down on all fours!

29 August 1985

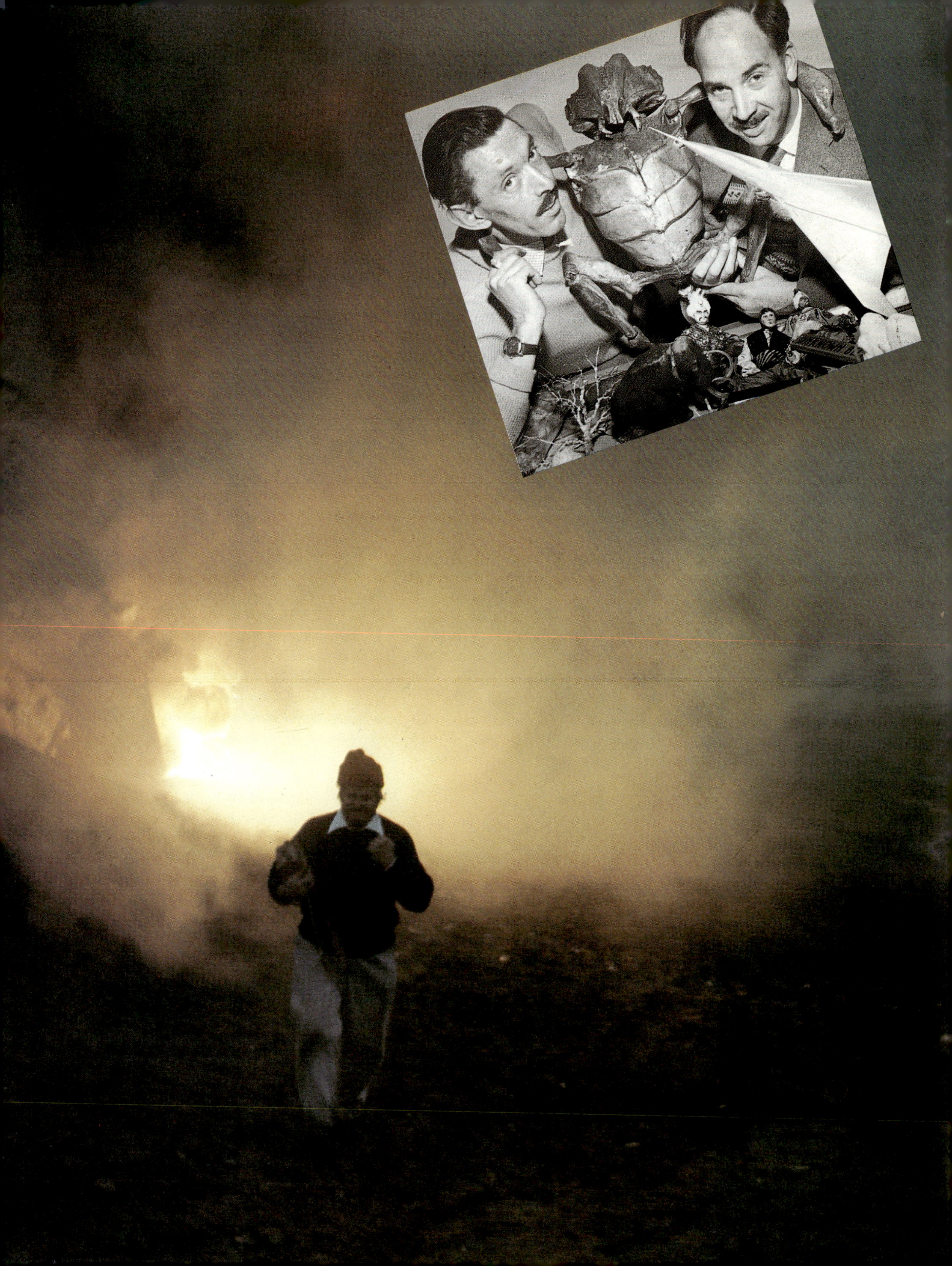

1
SPECIAL EFFECTS IN THE BEGINNING

IT WAS IN 1955 that two people who worked for BBC Television thought of creating a new department to make special effects for TV programmes. This particular art was not new. The film world, and the theatre, had been using effects for many years but, at that time, nobody did effects for television. So a small department was formed, which the BBC called the Visual Effects Department, in order not to confuse it with special *sound* effects. But whether you call them 'visual' or 'special', they are the same.

The creation of this new department brought together the perfect combination of visual effects people: an artist and an engineer. The artist was Jack Kine, a scenic artist who painted the backgrounds for television plays. Bernard Wilkie was the engineer, and he had been working at the BBC research centre on new television technology.

The first production for the new department was *Quatermass 2*. The hero, Professor Bernard Quatermass, was in some ways an early Doctor Who because, although based on Earth, he did find himself in some rather bizarre situations. The first story, *The Quatermass Experiment*, had been made a couple of years earlier, and features a strange creature that invades Westminster Abbey. It could have been the lack of a special department inside the BBC at that time that planted the idea in Jack and Bernard's minds of starting their own effects department. When it came to making *Quatermass 2*, the new Visual Effects Department had their work cut out devising and building the many effects for the programme. Pride of place goes to the finale where a creature grows inside oil refinery tanks in the

INSET LEFT **Jack Kine (left) and Bernard Wilkie, founders of the BBC Visual Effects Department with a Quatermass Martian.**

LEFT **The testing of pyrotechnics is very important. Here one of the heads of the BBC Visual Effects Department, Michaeljohn Harris, is calculating how near the explosion an actor can safely stand.**

estuary of the River Thames. Visual Effects supplied the miniature tanks, the creature and the final explosion.

From these small beginnings the department grew and grew. Models were built for *Blue Peter*; working demonstrations for schools' programmes and a series of highly improbable creations were made for a series called *It's a Square World*, which starred Michael Bentine and was really the forerunner of programmes like *The Goodies* and *Monty Python's Flying Circus*. Michael Bentine was famous for his creation of the Bumblies, which were a cross between one of the more bizarre Muppets and a hippopotamus. They spent most of their time hanging upside down from the ceiling, which should give you some idea of what the programme was like. Even today they would be fairly taxing for an Effects department.

The work in the new department was not always as unpredictable as that for Michael Bentine. The third Quatermass production, *Quatermass and the Pit*, gave the Visual Effects department even more work, and involved the designing of new creatures. This time it was Martians, and the story became one of the most successful TV plays ever produced. It was made in 1957, and although a cinema film was made in colour some years later, the original black-and-white TV version is still considered to be the better. I saw the complete story not so long ago, and the audience jumped out of their seats when the Martians first appeared – and suddenly moved!

Then, in the late 1960s a children's television series began,

BELOW **A model of the Rollrights stone circle from 'The Stones of Blood', used for one special effects shot that could not be achieved with the full size circle.**

which, though they did not know it at the time, was to become the most famous of all British science fiction series. This was, of course, *Doctor Who*.

Doctor Who was originally only planned as a six-part series, based around a rather crotchety old gentleman who travelled in a weird machine called a Tardis. His name came about because his real name was totally unpronounceable – by Earth people – and so when anyone said 'Doctor who?', he would usually reply 'Oh, that'll do … ! From the very beginning, the *Doctor Who* stories gave the Visual Effects Department a great deal of work and, probably more than any other programme, developed many of the skills needed to create effects.

At this point it is necessary to explain just what 'effects' are, for although I think that anyone who watches television or films knows what *they* mean by 'special effects', the name covers a wide, wide field.

Visual effects is the art of creating something that would not happen naturally, and it can touch on every aspect of the making of a television programme. However, effects can very generally be classified under three headings: special effects props, floor effects and, last but not least, models.

'Props' is short for 'properties', which in the theatrical world is anything that an actor uses during a performance. It could be the chair he sits on, the newspaper he reads, or the glass he drinks out of. They are all props, and they remain 'props' unless something special has to happen to them. The chair may have to collapse when sat on, or the newspaper catch fire. Possibly the glass will have to shatter. Then they stop being ordinary props and become effects props, because each one has to be specially made and prepared.

Floor effects is a term that covers a very wide range of effects. Fires, explosions and collapsing buildings are all floor effects, but so is everything to do with the weather. Rain, hail and snow all come under the heading of floor effects, for even in England you cannot guarantee that it will rain! Even if it is raining when you want it to, this will not usually show up on the film, so you have to add more water to make it look more like rain. The term 'floor effects' is used because the effects are worked while you are standing on the floor. The 'floor' can be the solid floor of a television studio, or the ground outside on location.

The third category of effects are models or, as they are so called, miniatures. This is the side of the work that people usually connect with visual effects, because it normally involves the creation of spaceships. But miniatures are far more than just the provision of model spaceships flying round the universe. Effects can supply in miniature any scene that would be difficult, or even impossible, to build full-size. These include alien landscapes and inaccessible areas of the Earth, like the Arctic, deserts and mountain regions.

It is possible to use real aircraft and ships in effects scenes, but it does tend to become very expensive, and possibly dangerous. Real aircraft have been blown up and ships sunk, but if a model is used the whole effect becomes more controll-

ABOVE **The Marconiscope built for 'The Pyramids of Mars' and worked by electric motors. It was blown up in the last episode.**

ABOVE **Miniature landscapes are often constructed for 'Doctor Who' to create alien planets. This scene was built for 'The City of Death'.**

able, safer and slightly cheaper (though not much!). But it is really with a scene in space that effects come into their own, as we cannot – yet – film real spacecraft 'in space'. For the time being we have to make do with models, and Doctor Who has met quite a few spaceships during his travels.

This, very simply, covers the three main areas of effects. Few effects fall squarely into one category, though. For instance, where models are made to explode, there is a combination of categories, since explosions are floor effects. And this state of affairs is quite normal in the department, for, whatever programme you are working on, there will always be something new, something that has not been done exactly that way before, so we are always breaking new ground. This applies to all the programmes that have used Visual Effects over the years: *Dad's Army*, *Blake's 7*, *Tomorrow's World*, *The Goodies*, *The Two Ronnies* and *The Tripods* – all have made great demands on the Visual Effects Department. But, over the thirty years the department has been in existence, one programme emerges as the most demanding: *Doctor Who*.

11

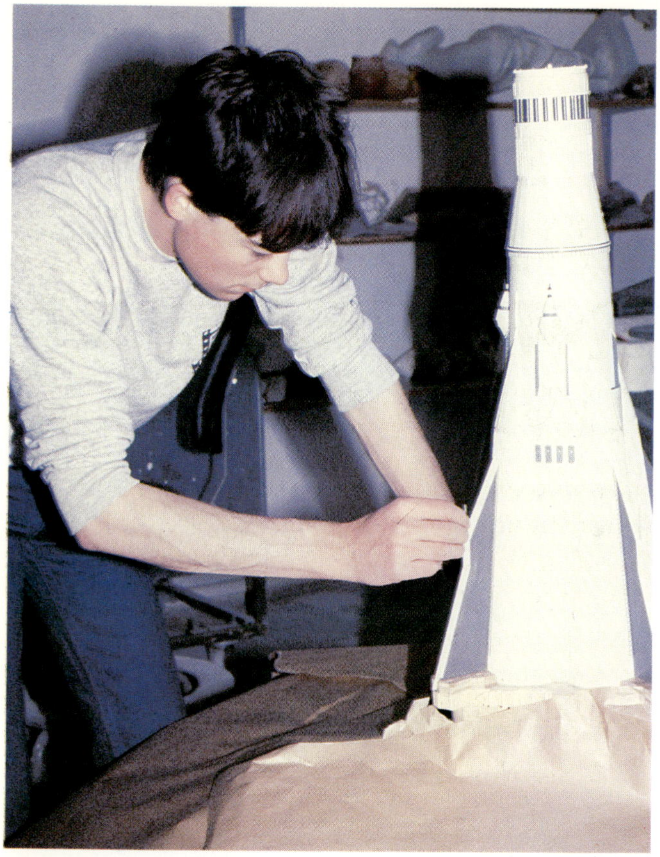

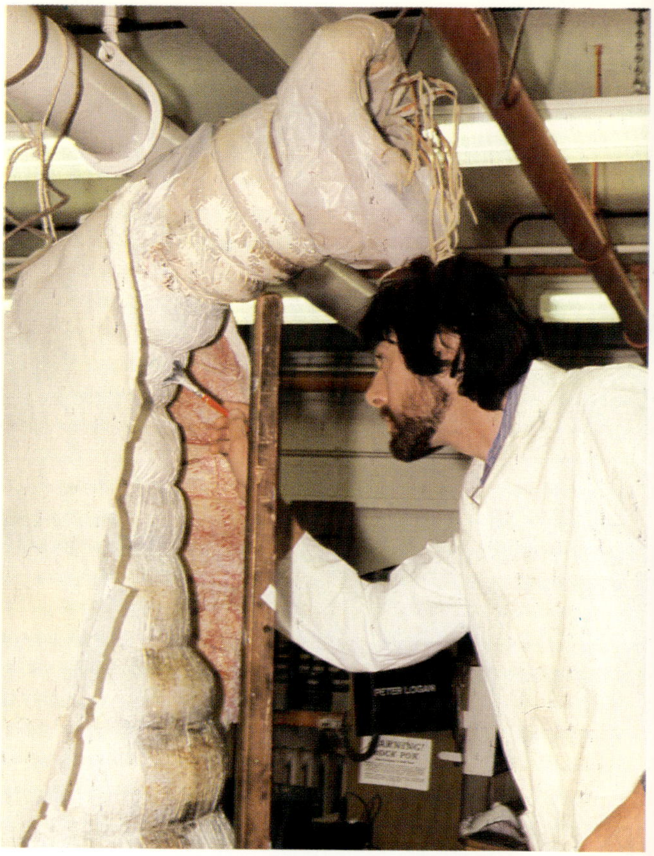
PETER LOGAN

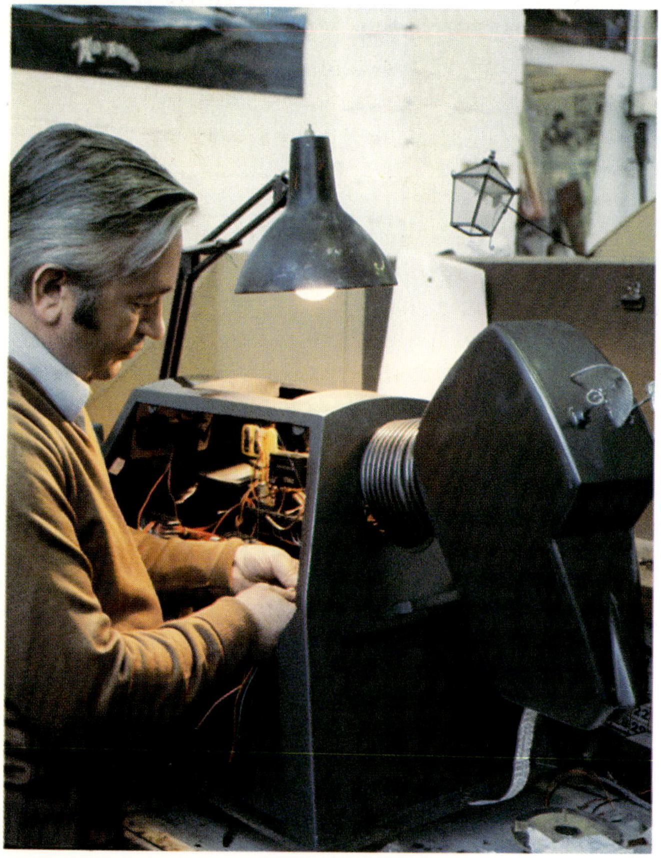

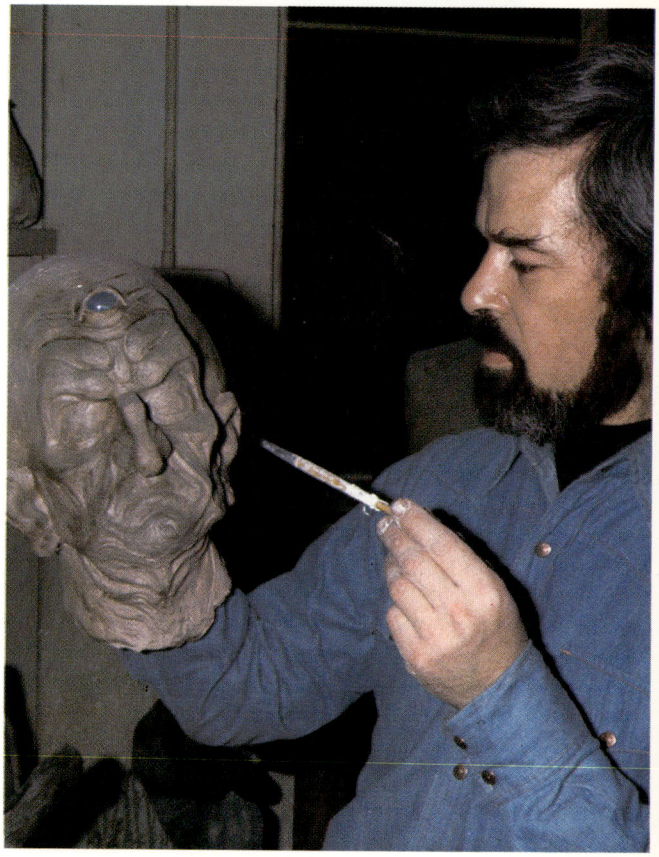

2
BEHIND THE SCENES ON 'DOCTOR WHO'

ALTHOUGH 'DOCTOR WHO' was originally made for children, it was never produced by the Children's Television Department. Instead, it has always been made by the Drama Series and Serials Department where programmes such as *Juliet Bravo*, *Bergerac*, *Tenko* and *The Tripods* are produced.

In overall charge of *Doctor Who* is the Producer, who decides what the style of the next season will be. He also commissions the scripts, and chooses the lead actors for each story. Working with the Producer is a Production Associate who has the unenviable task of attempting to keep track of all the money. There is also a Script Editor. Since each story is written by a different script writer it is necessary to have a Script Editor to ensure that the stories run together and that the Doctor is not asked to do something completely out of character. It is not unknown for the Script Editor to write at least one of the stories for each series.

The *Doctor Who* programmes are actually made by a production team. There is a different team, headed by a Director, for each story. The main reason for this is that there is no way that one team could make all six *Doctor Who* stories in any one series. It takes over four months to finish a single story, so you would need a 24-month year to complete all six – and that's without a holiday! So each story is made as a separate television drama, and there is no connection between the people working on one story and those working on the next, except of course for the Producer, Production Associate and Script Editor.

There are, not surprisingly, a large number of people in-

ABOVE FAR LEFT **Stuart Murdoch working on the model rocket used in the story 'State of Decay'.**

ABOVE LEFT **Colin Mapson creates the creatures from 'Image of the Fendahl' using foam and rubber.**

BELOW FAR LEFT **Charlie Lumm repairs the wiring for the Mark III K-9 ready for 'K-9 and Company'.**

BELOW LEFT **John Friedlander with the original Davros mask moulded in rubber.**

volved in the making of a *Doctor Who*, or any other television programme. Besides the Director, about half a dozen people make up the Production Team. Other people are then assigned to help that team, including those from Visual Effects.

Visual Effects is part of a larger group known as Design. There are five groups in Design which deal with the design of the sets: the Designer, the Graphics Designer (who designs lettering, art-work, or, in the case of a new programme, the titles), the Costume Designer, the Make-up Designer and, last but by no means least, the Visual Effects Designer. For most television programmes, these designers work closely together on many aspects of the production, but nowhere is this truer than in the case of *Doctor Who*. The Visual Effects Designer especially needs to work very closely with all his designer colleagues as many of the effects elements for a *Doctor Who* story will overlap with items being made by one or another of the design groups.

Visual Effects Designers, like myself, are responsible for creating, designing and supervising the manufacture of effects. We do not, as a rule, get down to making them ourselves, although most of us like to get our hands dirty at some point, pitching in to help our assistants.

The Visual Effects Design Assistants are very important to the production as they actually construct all the special effects props, models and devices used to create the effects. No effect is ever repeated exactly, so virtually everything has to be made for each programme. A small amount of equipment is kept as 'stock', including items to create fires and explosions, and devices for dropping lightweight materials from the ceiling – but even these are invariably adapted in some way before they can be used.

There is no set number of Assistants to a Designer for a *Doctor Who* programme. Every story is assessed individually and the number of Assistants assigned accordingly. Many years ago, *Doctor Who* programmes were occasionally made by just one Designer. This would never happen now. Today, on average, the basic effects team consists of the Designer and three or four Assistants, one of whom is a Senior Assistant who takes over when the Designer is absent. The Assistants form the core of the work force, but the Effects Designer can also call on additional help and specialists when necessary.

We always say 'we don't specialise' in the Effects Department as everyone is potentially capable of doing anything! But when it comes to, say, a complicated electronic circuit for a new radio communicator prop, or possibly the moulded head for a monster, we have specialists within the department who are able to do these items quickly and efficiently. There are also people outside the BBC who build effects items for us. These are freelance contractors and there are a large number of them all over the country, working on films, television commercials, theatre plays, exhibitions, and effects required by independent TV companies, which do not have a built-in effects department like the BBC. Knowing that some items go outside to these contractors, a list is kept detailing which contractor is best suited to each type of work. Outside contractors tend to specialise more in one or more aspect of effects work, so there are specialist prop makers, model makers and electricians.

I said we do not specialise in the Effects Department and this is really the essence of our work, for you never know what you will be doing next. One day you may be building an intricate model out of a variety of plastic parts, and the next carefully welding a structure to support the model for filming. Some people, of course, like one type of work more than another. If an Assistant has studied sculpture at Art College for instance and a *Doctor Who* programme needs a new creature's head, that particular Assistant is going to enjoy that particular job. Sometimes the work is not quite so artistic. A new weapon may have been designed and a prototype made. Then another dozen are needed, so a kind of short assembly line has to be set up to manufacture all the bits necessary and put together the weapon collection. This can get a bit tedious, but has to be done. I can remember, many years ago, having to construct thirty fake logs for a fire sequence. These logs had to be made so that they would not burn. I spent days up to my elbows in water, breaking up a fire-proof material, then cutting chicken wire and wrapping it round to form the frames. I then plastered the wire with the mushy mix, creating a log pattern, and allowed the logs to dry. Finally, I painted them. This was all in a day's – or rather a week's – work. We still have a few of the logs in our store, so perhaps it was all worthwhile!

ABOVE **Julian Fullalove and Martin Geeson road-test the buggy designed by Charlie Jeanes for 'Vengeance on Varos'.**

3
PLANNING EFFECTS

THE FIRST STAGE in any *Doctor Who* story is the script, without which we would all sit round and twiddle our thumbs! All the people involved in the production receive a set of scripts to read before the first production meeting. The script provides the story with all its twists, turns and sub-plots, and possibly some details of where the scenes are to be set. It may also give details of specific creatures or props that Effects will be dealing with, though this is the exception rather than the rule. The script we first see may or may not be the 'final' version. Normally at this stage it is a 'draft script', but things do not usually change all that drastically – you hope!

When I first read 'Warriors' Gate' it was not 'Warriors' Gate' at all but 'The Dream Time'. It is not unknown for the title of a *Doctor Who* story to change. 'Meglos' was originally 'The Last Zolfa Thuran' and 'The Wasting' turned into 'State of Decay'.

My first impression of 'Warriors' Gate' was that here was a *Doctor Who* that was a bit different. As it turned out it was one of the oddest *Doctor Who*s ever made. Having read the storyline, I look at the overall setting of a story: whether any models are mentioned, what special effects props appear, and what location filming is involved.

Location scenes are normally filmed before studio scenes, so one thing I have to think about is whether any effects for location have to be created first. I also have to take into account any mention of models and miniatures as it is my job as Effects Designer to deal with all the models, deciding when it is best to film or video-record them.

Models and location aside, the majority of any *Doctor Who*

production takes place in a television studio using electronic cameras. This is by far the quickest way to make any TV programme, drama or otherwise. The Director has four or five cameras at his disposal. Using video cameras as opposed to film, the Director can see what he is recording and, if necessary, play it back to make sure that he has what he wants. With film, normally only one camera is used, and you have to wait until the next day at the earliest to see the 'rushes' and to discover whether they are exactly what you wanted, and whether the film has developed properly. More and more 'film' television dramas are now being made with lightweight TV cameras, including *Doctor Who*. Film still has its place, though, as many people prefer the 'look' of film as opposed to videotape, and many directors still prefer to work with film.

All these details were going through my mind as I read the script of 'Warriors' Gate'. It was an odd *Doctor Who* in that it did not have a location, so there were no effects that took priority. I soon realized, however, that a large percentage of the story was set in a 'nothing', but even 'nothing' has to be 'something' for *Doctor Who*, so I knew that this was something which would involve effects. . . .

I make notes in a script as I go, putting a double red line

BELOW **The Banqueting Hall from 'Warriors' Gate'. Doctor Who (Tom Baker) examines a lifeless Gundan robot, while K-9 sits on a cobweb-covered table. Both the TV camera and the sound boom can be seen.**

against what looks like an effects sequence, so that I can look at it in detail later. 'Warriors' Gate' became full of double red lines, for if it was not our 'nothing', the action concerned a spaceship (the Privateer) or the Gate of the title, both of which were going to involve effects. And to these were added all the other items that pop up in any *Doctor Who* episode: weapons, radio communicators, electrical panels, large special props that have to 'do' something – the list goes on and on. In this story, too, one of the Doctor's companions was that funny-looking metallic box on wheels – K-9.

I finally end up with a list of effects. This list, or lists, will run from episode to episode, and detail separately the special effects props, the floor effects and where I think I will need to liaise with fellow designers in other design groups. The models and miniatures are taken out and listed separately as they will be dealt with separately. Where necessary, I also try to note if items will be continuing from episode to episode. Although some effects are used just the once, many appear on and off throughout the whole story, such as K-9. Armed with this pile of papers, the next stage is a planning meeting. The first such planning meeting for any *Doctor Who* involves almost everyone and 'Warriors' Gate' was no exception.

The Director is there, and the Producer and the Script Editor (though not the Script Writer, since once the script has been accepted that is the last he or she sees of it!). All the production team attend, and all the Designers, the Set Designer, Make-up and Costume, the Electronic or Video Effects Operator who will be creating most of the electronic tricks in the programme, and of course myself as Visual Effects Designer.

Then follows the task of going through the script and sorting out exactly what it is all about, and who is doing what. The Director will have firm ideas of what he sees as the overall style of a story. The Director of 'Warriors' Gate', Paul Joyce, had his own thoughts about the Gate, but left the Privateer to myself and the Set Designer, Graeme Story.

This was a classic case of Effects and Scenic Design cooperating, as Graeme had to provide the full-size interior of the ship, where the actors would be working, while I would design and have made the exterior of the ship as a model. Obviously the styles had to match. There was no point in Graeme designing an interior that would have put the bridge of the USS Enterprise to shame, if I came up with something that looked as if it had escaped from Steptoe's backyard. Luckily we knew that the Privateer was, to put it kindly, somewhat old and weary as spaceships go. It was a ship, probably initially from Earth, that roamed the Time Winds, trying to make a fast buck. The Privateer was therefore a somewhat tatty craft, and both Graeme and myself had this in mind while designing.

The crew of the Privateer were also a tatty lot, including a Laurel-and-Hardy-like duo played by Freddie Earle and Harry Waters. They were not the only occupants of the Privateer. Captured and used as navigators along the Time Winds were a race of lion-like humanoids, the Tharils. Now, as soon as a monster is mentioned in *Doctor Who*, it is invariably time for co-operation with fellow designers. In the case of the Tharils and the other creatures of 'Warriors' Gate', the Gundan robots, this did not immediately involve Visual Effects. Instead, the Costume Designer, June Hudson, and the Make-up Designer, Pauline Cox, did most of this work. Visual Effects only came into it when something 'special' had to happen – for example, when the Gundan had his head knocked off!

Even if there were not creatures to worry about in this particular story, there was always the 'nothing'. This became a co-operation between Scenic, Visual and Electronic Effects in the guise of the Electronic Effects Operator, Robin Lobb. The easy way out of the 'nothing' was a white background, but a white studio does not stay white for very long, and Graeme would have great difficulty hiding the join between the 'floor' and the 'wall' of the studio. It was soon decided that the only way to produce this effect was to overlay it electronically on to the picture by the Colour Separation Overlay method. I should explain about CSO, for it features very widely in television. The process is also known by the trade name Chromakey, but the two processes and the final effect are the same.

ABOVE **The control desk of the Video Effects workshop which creates all types of electronic effects. The bank of TV screens shows how the pictures are built up, stage by stage.**

CSO relies on the fact that a television picture is built up from only three colours. They are red, green and blue and are known as the primary light colours. Combining any of the colours together in varying proportions creates all the other colours, so the whole spectrum can be shown on a television screen. The three colours are picked up by three corresponding video tubes in the television camera, one that picks up only the red light, one the green, and one the blue. The way CSO works is to replace one of these colours with another picture and the normal colour used is blue.

The idea first began as a way to put a picture within the whole picture for news broadcasts. The newsreader would be seated at the desk, while over his or her shoulder there would be a picture of whatever was being discussed. If you were actually to go into that TV news studio while this was going on, you would not see the photograph behind the newsreader's shoulder, only a bright blue panel. The camera looking at the scene also 'sees' only this blue panel, but electronically the blue is replaced with the appropriate photograph. This then is CSO in its simplest form.

It was not too long, though, before producers of drama plays realized that if a background could be replaced so easily for the news, there was no reason why an actor could not be put into a location in the same way, as it is not necessary to use a still

1

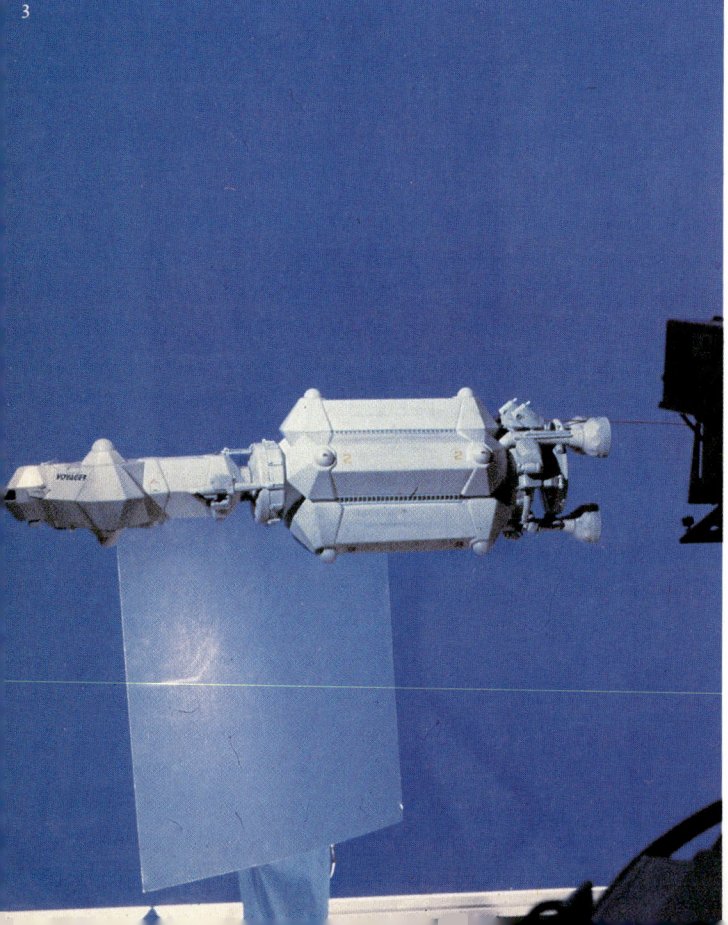

2

3

4

LEFT **A sequence of pictures from 'Galloping Galaxies' which show how Colour Separation Overlay works. In** 1, **the spaceship Voyager stands in front of the CSO blue background. CSO blue card is placed in front of the Voyager's stand to mask it. Then the TV camera on the right records the scene. At the same time,** 2, **the background of stars, is 'keyed' into the picture, replacing all the blue colour. The video tape can then be replayed and a second spaceship,** 3, **is keyed into the scene. The final picture can be seen in** 4 – **two spacecrafts floating against a background of stars.**

photograph for CSO – a film, videotape or even another camera's picture in the same studio could be used. So an actor could be walking along the streets of Paris, climbing a pyramid, or standing in an alien landscape, all without moving from the television studio, and all through using CSO.

Of course it is not quite as easy as I have made it sound, because to make somebody appear realistically to be in another location, it is not just a case of standing them against the blue CSO colour. The lighting on them must match the background, and the angle of the camera must also match. It is no use looking up at the person if the background view has been shot looking downwards!

I said at the beginning of this explanation that the colour usually used for CSO was blue, but any colour can in fact be used, and for the studio of 'Warriors' Gate', the colour chosen to key the CSO was green. The reason behind this, if you have not already guessed, is the Tardis.

The Tardis is blue, albeit a dark shade, and although it is not impossible to 'key' this colour against CSO blue, it is not all that straightforward. So green was chosen instead. This however meant that green was a colour that had to be avoided on all the costumes, props and anything else that might appear in the 'nothing' and hence against the green CSO colour.

So what may appear a simple matter is in fact very complicated and involves virtually all the design team. Even then it was not complete, for we decided that something more than a plain white sheet of card was needed to give a more even look to the whole 'nothing'. So I built a hemisphere of perspex, which was spray-painted white, and lit from the outside. It was this 'white nothing' that was eventually overlayed into the green area to give the final effect.

This then was just the first of many planning meetings. Each time, I went away armed with more and more information, and more and more problems to try and sort out before our first session in the studio.

4
CONSTRUCTING EFFECTS

AN EFFECTS LIST for a *Doctor Who* studio looks fairly impressive, and with 'Warriors' Gate', like most *Doctor Who*s, the overriding problem was how we were going to complete everything in time. The lead-up to filming a *Doctor Who* is only two months, which is not a long time for a four-part story.

'Warriors' Gate' required guns and communicators for the Privateer crew, some of which needed to 'work', or at least look as if they were working. There was also a large MZ Laser Cannon (which played an important part in the last episode), and an electronic pack that crew-member Lane carried everywhere to give details of the crew's surroundings. The floor effects consisted of the following, several instances of electrical panels exploding and catching fire, the gateway blowing up at the end; K-9 having to be repaired by Romana, and crewman Sagan being killed by a Tharil using a high-voltage cable.

Problem number one, though, was how to get the manufacture of all the effects props started. This was an 'assembly line' job, for we needed several of both the guns and the communicators. The difficulties with both these types of effects props is that they get a lot of use in a studio and are liable to break, so they need to be as strong as possible. Unfortunately, the stronger they are, the heavier, so there has to be some sort of compromise. One good material to use is called cold-cast resin. It is the same sort of resin as that used to make car body repairs, and if metal powder is mixed with it, you end up with a substance that looks and feels like metal, is very strong, but is not all that heavy. It was ideal for the guns, so I got one of my contractors to do the job. I gave him a pattern for the gun (based on a gun design from an earlier programme) with detailed instructions and the idea of using cold-cast resin.

RIGHT **The Doctor (Tom Baker) builds a Beam Machine watched by the Professor (Beatrix Lehmann). Supposedly concocted from bits and pieces, the machine was really a special effects prop built around a photographic tripod.**

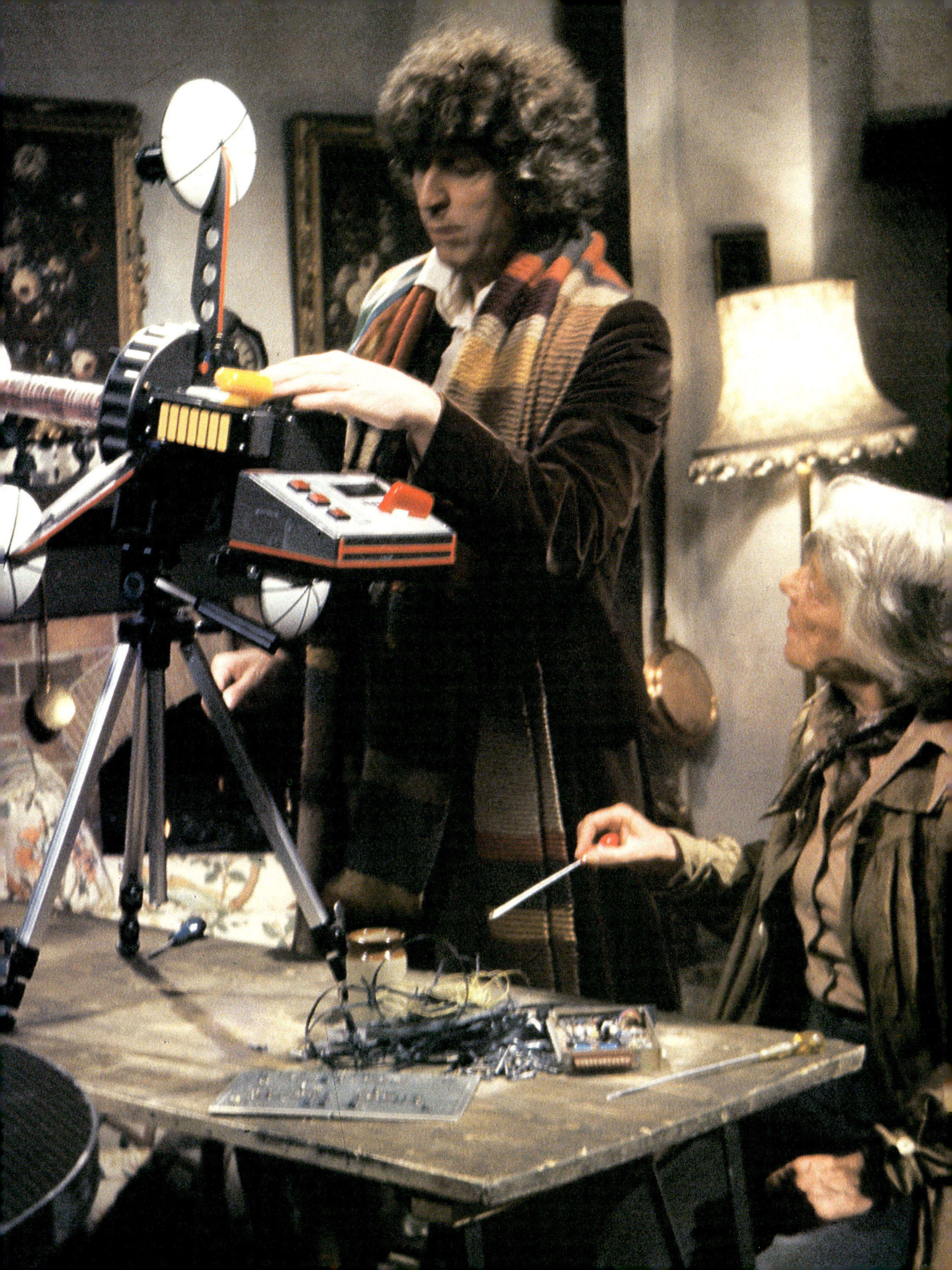

Unfortunately, something got lost in the communication for, when the guns arrived, they were not made from cold-cast metal resin, but from solid metal! Consequently, we did not break one, though they were rather heavy! In fact at one point they nearly broke the set. The actor Kenneth Cope, who played the Privateer crewman Packard, approached the Tardis in one scene and had to tap his gun on the side of the police box to see what it was. The Tardis as a piece of scenery is not all that strong, nothing like as strong as the solid metal guns, so when Ken bashed the side with the gun, the Tardis visibly rocked! In the end, although we used the metal guns for the close-ups, we had to compromise and make some plastic copies for the crew to put in their holsters, otherwise they would all have been walking around lop-sided.

The communicators that the crew use to talk to one another in the story did not have to be quite as strong. A small electronic device was built into a few of them that flashed some

BELOW **Some special effects props from 'Doctor Who' and 'Blake's 7'. Top left is the gun for 'The Face of Evil', the Gundan axe is next to it and the Liberator gun bottom right.**

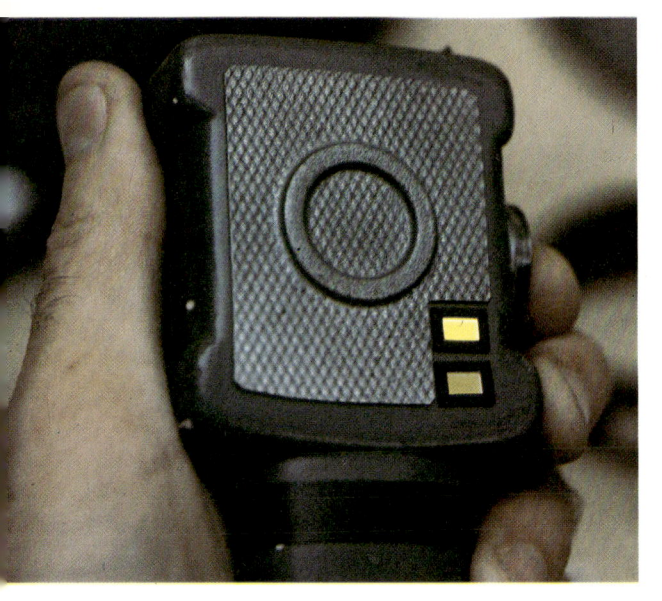

ABOVE LEFT **The Privateer communicator from 'Warriors' Gate', with one of the two yellow lights emitting diodes, glowing. This was operated by the actor's forefinger on a side switch.**

ABOVE RIGHT **Here you see the large '100 Imperials' coin specially cast from metal for 'Warriors' Gate'. Compare its size to the Churchill crown on the right.**

light-emitting diodes when switched on. It did not mean anything, but it looked as if something was happening. The real problem with this kind of prop was that the actors kept losing them. Because the communicators were relatively small, they carried them in their pockets and, at the end of a recording when the actors left the studio, so did all the communicators! By the next day, most were lost, having fallen out of pockets at inopportune moments. Experience taught me to build at least double the number required.

Another story I worked on, 'Warriors of the Deep', also had radio communicators, and in even greater quantities than 'Warriors' Gate'. In this case there were over two dozen, four of which worked in the flashing-light style. Luckily, I had now learnt to keep lots in reserve for when one got lost or broken. For in the end there were so many being used at one time that I had to have the assembly line actually going in the studio to ensure there were enough for everyone! It certainly worked and we never kept the studio waiting for more than a few seconds while a communicator was replaced.

These effects props, where several are needed, are one example of work that can be sent 'outside' to a contractor to be manufactured. The special prop, where only one is required, is usually kept inside the Department.

27

The largest effects prop in 'Warriors' Gate' was the MZ Laser Cannon. It was a device with a big dish at one end, a seat at the other, and a wheel at each corner which made steering very difficult. There were also a lot of mechanical bits and pieces in between. As far as the story went, its exact function was not clear, though the Privateer crew attempted to blast down the mirrors used by the Tharils to travel between 'times' with it. Unfortunately, they only succeeded in showering themselves with rubble. If the MZ only really got used at the end of the story, it did have a use throughout most of the story as a hiding-place. The MZ is conveniently covered with a blanket while in storage, and this proved a useful hiding-place for Romana, Adric and K-9 or, on one occasion, all three! The cover was made from several of those shiny survival blankets campers and hikers tend to use nowadays, which looked suitably 'science fiction'. Unfortunately, when we got into the studio and Romana, Adric and K-9 were climbing about under it, one overriding problem became apparent: the blankets rustled! Eventually, we had to glue black cloth all over the underside of the blanket in an attempt to cut down the noise. It helped slightly, but not a lot, and we all hoped that whoever was underneath would keep as still as possible and therefore keep the rustling noises to a minimum.

The MZ gun itself had to be built from the ground up. Because it was going to have to take the weight of several of the cast, including K-9, it needed a solid metal chassis. This was made from welded steel tube, rather like the backbone of a racing car, with a large castor fixed to each corner. The dish of the laser cannon part was a large perspex shape and the seat at the other end started life as an office chair that just happened to have fallen apart. In between was fixed an air-ram to raise the dish part (though this feature was not eventually used) and provision was made on board for the air bottle which worked the ram as well. As I knew there would be at least one person inside it and possibly K-9, it was made possible for the actors to grab and hold various bits of mechanism along each side, while the MZ was being wheeled. K-9 conveniently fitted on the flattest part of the metal-work, otherwise he would have had to be strapped in every time.

Besides these large items, there are many smaller ones that come under Effects mainly because there is no other way to obtain them. One rather interesting effects prop for 'Warriors' Gate' was a coin. Not the most exciting of props you might think, but this one was going to be involved in at least two effects sequences. It had to be a large coin and I originally volunteered the loan of one of my own crowns, but even this was not really large enough. In the end, we decided to make our own '100 Imperials', and they were produced by the same method as the guns, although this time we intended them to be solid metal. The coin is used by the two comic members of the crew who flip it in the air at the exact time the ship starts to move through the Time Winds. The coin stops in mid-air and seems to hang in space. Then the ship returns to normal – well, almost normal – and all the electrical control panels explode (more effects), and the coin falls slowly, spinning and turning, to the deck. It is a straightforward-looking scene when viewed, but it took a lot of setting up and recording, and I spent ages practising spinning the coin so that it would fall and spin realistically. Not the easiest of tasks for a coin that is nearly 60 mm in diameter.

Strangely enough, this way of making solid metal objects was used for a third time in 'Warriors' Gate'. The Gundam robots carried axes, and for one scene one of these had to thud into the solid wooden table that dominated the banqueting-hall inside the gateway. Normally this type of axe or weapon would be made from wood, or fibreglass, but neither would be strong enough to be smashed into the table. So two of the axes were made of solid metal, although the remainder were ordinary fibreglass. This made the former more than strong enough to hit the wood, and to gouge their way through without damage to the axe. The table did not come off so well. In the studio I did the swinging of the axe myself and it was an exhilarating feeling to bring it smashing down on the table!

By the time all these bits and pieces were designed and built there was quite a collection ready for the first recording, and the next worry was assembling everything ready for transportation to the studio, hoping nothing had been forgotten!

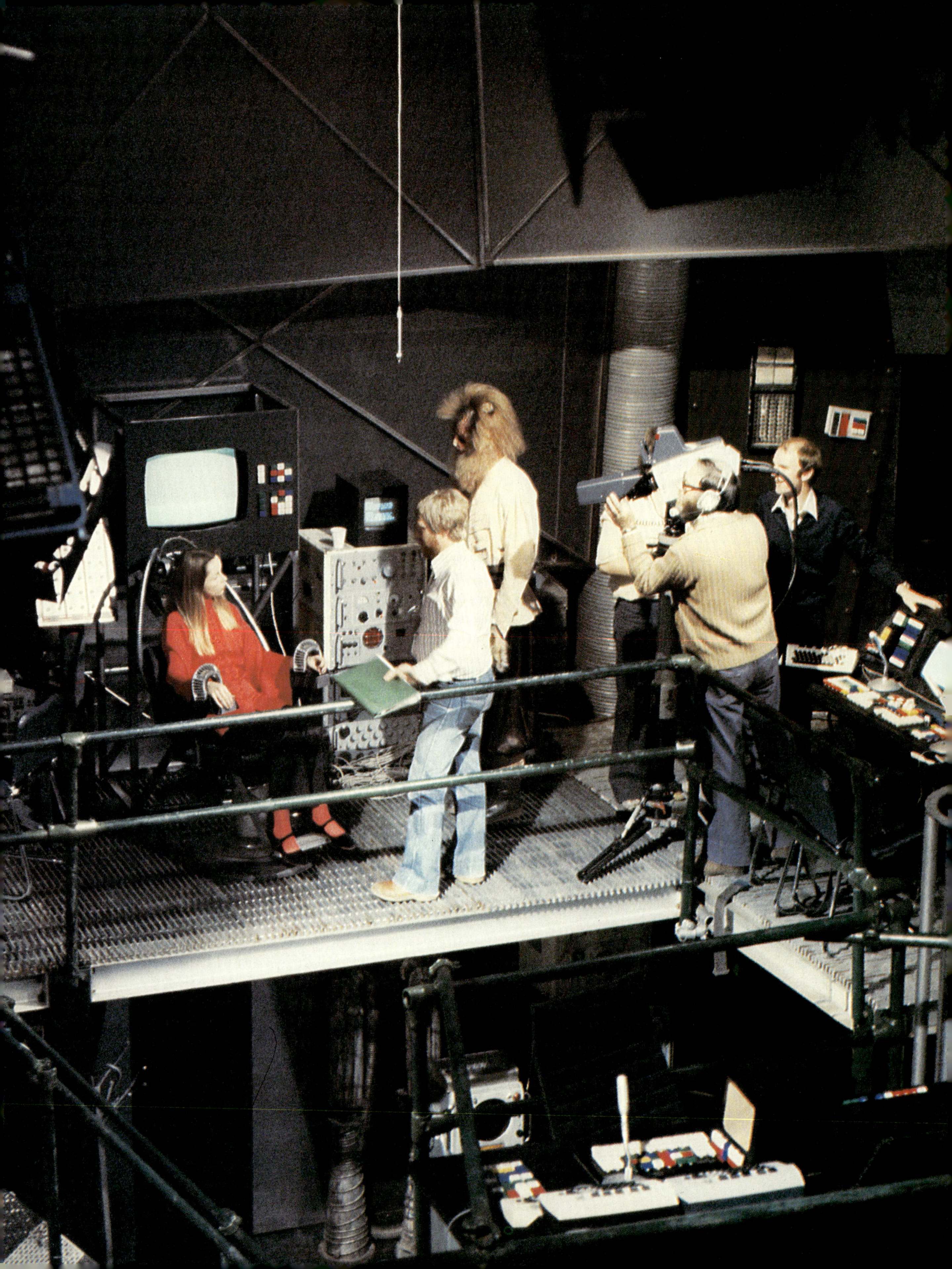

5
'DOCTOR WHO' AND THE TV STUDIO

IF YOU HAVE never been in a television studio before, first sight can be very impressive. Hundreds of lamps hang precariously overhead, while cables snake across the floor just waiting to trip you up. The majority of television programmes are made in these purpose-built studios, as everything is to hand and more or less under control.

Getting ready to go into the studio to make a *Doctor Who*, I ensure that I have everything I and my team will need for the next two or three days. Three days is the longest a *Doctor Who* is ever in one studio at a time, so to record the five days needed for a story, filming is split between a two and three-day session. Into the studio go all the scenery, cameras, microphones, props, costumes and, of course, all the Visual Effects paraphernalia. Because the Visual Effects Workshop is no longer on the Television Centre site, everything has to be packed up and transported there. You can rush back to the workshop in the lunch break if you really need to (and we invariably do have to), but you try to avoid this if humanly possible.

Apart from the specially made props, like the guns, communicators and the MZ Laser Cannon, 'Warriors' Gate' needed several of the items held in stock. For the explosion scenes, I needed dropping boxes which could be hung overhead, and filled with lightweight dust and rubble to drop onto the Privateer crew. For the same scene I needed Woofers – large tanks full of compressed air – which can blow the same sort of rubble from the floor area. These are very large and heavy, and as we only have a few of them for all the programmes, it is a stock effects item I have to remember to book

LEFT **The bridge of the Privateer spaceship built in the TV studio. A small hand-held TV camera can be seen in the centre, ready to take a picture of Romana and the Tharil.**

well in advance. Otherwise, I find someone else has booked them and they are on location in Scotland!

So, on the morning of the first studio day, the area around the Assistants' benches begins to look like a scene from a jumble sale. All the effects props have been got together, carefully packed in a way they will never be again. The stock effects clutter one corner, while large boxes, called studio boxes, occupy another. These contain all the items and bits and pieces that there does not seem the remotest possibility of using, but which will get used some day, and that could be today. So you have to take them with you. There are also large supplies of glues, nails, paint and tools with which to mend the effects props should they fall apart in the studio. For 'Warriors' Gate', K-9 had to be made to work, and for this particular story I had the additional problem that his usual operator, Nigel Brackley, had broken his ankle. Although he had gallantly offered to hobble in, I had said that I would operate the dog myself. Although we did not know it at the time, this was to be the last appearance of K-9 Mark 2 in a *Doctor Who* story. The Tardis console also had to be moved out of storage, and transported to the studio.

So all the items were packed on board our Visual Effects van for transporting just down the road to the Television Centre and the *Doctor Who* studio. Unpacking is almost as traumatic as packing, for this time there is the problem of where it is all going to go. Any studio is always full of scenery and trying to find an odd corner where the gear can be stored safely, where you can get at it and where, if necessary, you can repair it, is a headache an Effects Designer can do without. The trouble is that everyone else is having the same problem, and as soon as you think you have located a little niche, you find a camera has to pass through there, so you have to move.

'Warriors' Gate' only had three sets, apart from the Tardis interior, but they were all large. Other *Doctor Who*s can have as many as seven or eight small sets. The interior of the Privateer was built on two levels and was so high that in some scenes you could see the girders at the top of the studio. However, as they looked very similar to the framework of the ship, this did not matter too much. The area that was supposedly behind the Gateway was the Banqueting Hall, which was also large, and had a first-floor balcony running round two sides. I should point out that these two sets were not in the same studio at the same time, for each alone took up a fair-sized area. But of course the largest set for 'Warriors' Gate' was the 'nothing' and this was immediately visible as soon as you walked into the studio as a vast expanse of bright CSO green. The floor was painted green and a large green cloth, called a cyclorama or 'cyc', stretched around the outside of this area. In the green area stood three full-sized pieces of scenery that I was also supplying as models. There was the Tardis itself; the airlock part of the Privateer, and the lower part of the Gateway.

Television studio days are long, usually thirteen hours at a time. We used only actually to record in the evening – the rest of the day was spent in rehearsals. Gradually, we began to record in the afternoon and now the common practice is to 'rehearse-record', which means you rehearse a sequence, then record it while it is still fresh in everyone's mind. A four-part *Doctor Who* takes five long studio days to record, plus the location time, if there is any, the model filming time and a special electronic effects day – and this is before the Director starts to edit. This may sound a lot, but for a complicated

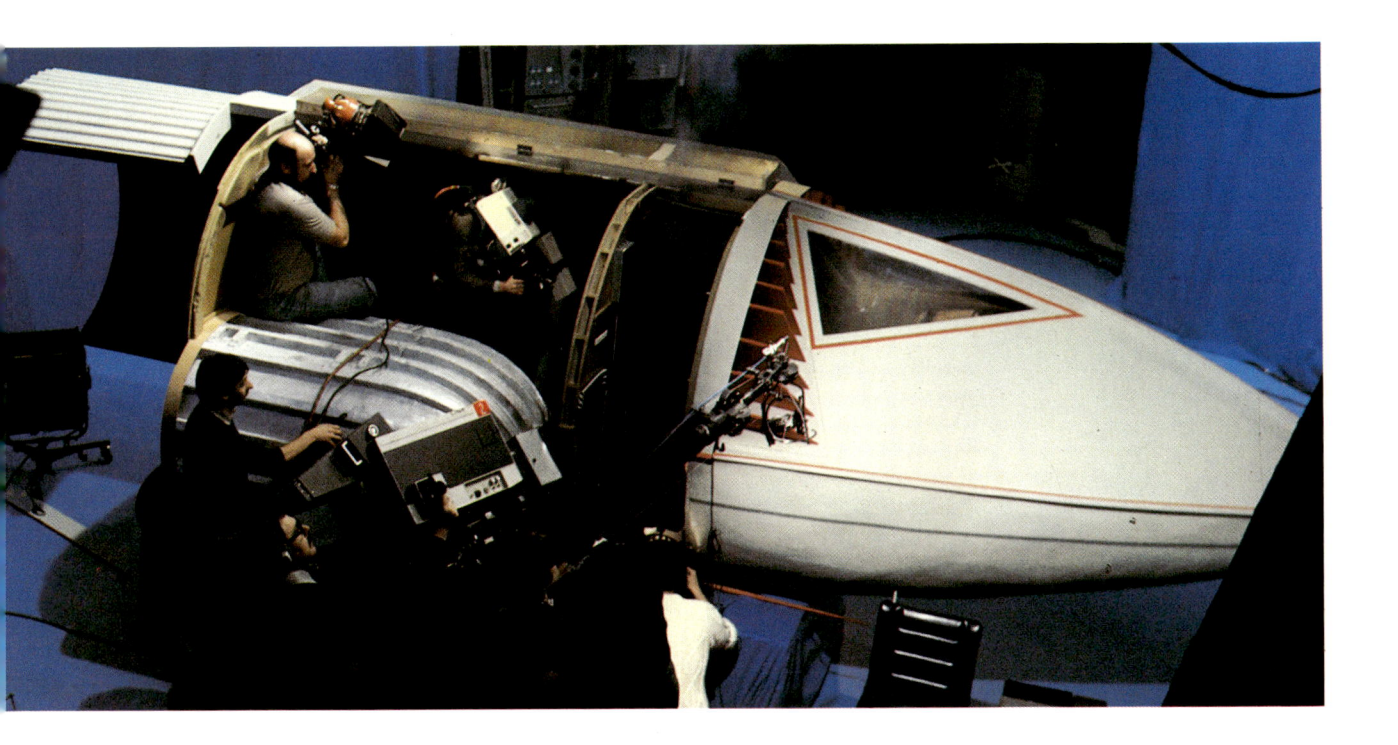

BELOW **Fire on board ship in 'Blake's 7.' The white spaceship is set against the blue CSO background and there are two cameras, microphones, lights and an Effects Assistant ready with a smoke gun.**

programme like *Doctor Who* it is not really that long, and it would be even longer if everything was shot on film.

Once into the studio, the first task of the effects team was to fit any item that would become part of the scenery, such as the control panels. The wiring to the panels then had to be carefully led away to a convenient spot, where it would later be wired into switches and battery packs. The actors then had to be issued with their guns and communicators and shown how they worked. Items like the coin had to be kept safely as there were only two. In fact, 'Warriors' Gate' proved a good rehearsal for 'Warriors of the Deep' as far as these special effects props were concerned, as for the latter I had to provide twenty-four communicators, twelve rifles, six hand-guns, fourteen electronic panels, three Silurian communicators and seven Sea Devil weapons. In the end I had to use one Assistant specifically to issue everything in the mornings and check everything in at the end of the studio day.

Another part of my job is to ensure that where effects have to explode or collapse, nothing goes wrong and injures someone. Though the Gateway had to be seen to explode at the end of 'Warriors' Gate', this was all filmed as a model and so was not a problem. There was, however, the earlier sequence (mentioned above) where the Privateer's crew attempt to use the MZ to blast through the mirrors – and here the cast were involved with the actual explosion and the collapse of rubble. It happened inside the full-sized gateway, which I rigged with the dropping boxes above and the two Woofers at either side. This sent out a shower of dust and lightweight materials which, even if any did hit anyone, would not do them any harm. Even so I still had to be very careful before I committed myself to pushing the button that released all this chaos. I had to be sure that everyone was in their correct place, that nobody had moved where they should not and that everyone was aware of what was about to happen. I then told the Production Assistant (now the Production Manager) that I was happy, the videotape machine started, and I pushed the button.

One snag with this type of explosive effect is that it creates a lot of mess which then has to be cleared up when the habitual cry comes down from the Director, 'Can we do that again, please?' I was lucky with this particular scene in that I only had to do it once. This was because we had thoughtfully remembered to have *two* video recorders running, each recording a different scene. In the normal course of events there are two video recorders running anyway, but they both record exactly the same. The idea behind this is that should anything go wrong with one machine, and it is not discovered at the time, it will be on the other machine. (We trust that we do not lose two machines at the same time!) It can also be slightly quicker when it comes to the editing if the Director has two original tapes rather than one. But in exceptional circumstances, like some effects sequences, it is possible to switch the camera outputs so that each video machine records a different picture. It is not often done, but it is a useful trick and can save time.

For the Privateer panels and wiring that had to smoulder and catch fire, I used very small pyrotechnic devices, rather like special fireworks. They were twisted around the existing panels or scenery, and then ignited by an electric fuse which spluttered and smoked like wiring burning itself out. Very small gunpowder packs can then add individual puffs and bangs at appropriate points. All these are very carefully placed in position, away from any of the cast, who have anyway been forewarned. If necessary I take them through a rehearsal with the pyrotechnic effects first, using myself or one of the Assistants as a stand-in. Once they are perfectly happy with what's going to happen, the effects are re-set and the recording can begin. At one point in 'Warriors' Gate' there was Clifford Rose, who played Rorvik, the Captain of the Privateer, Lalla Ward as Romana and Tom Baker as the Doctor, all hanging off the girders and wiring of the ship, which was smoking and spluttering away, and all this three metres above the studio floor.

Sometimes the Effects team take the actors' parts when pyrotechnics are involved, and there was one occasion like this in 'Warriors' Gate'. Near the end of the story, one of the crew, Sagan, attempts to revive one of the Tharils to use as a new navigator. However, he is attacked by one of the other Tharils and electrocuted with a supposedly high-tension cable. I decided that it would be easier if we did this particular scene, and not the actors, as it would only be seen very close up. I played Sagan, and one of my assistants, Simon Tayler (now himself an Effects Designer) played the Tharil. Sagan has to be electrocuted in the chest, so I used one of the metal bullet-hit plates we have in stock for 'shooting' people. Over this went one of the T-shirts that matched what the crew wore, and one of their bright orange overalls. Simon meanwhile wore the furry lion-like skin of the Tharils on one arm and hand. He had a bunch of lethal-looking cables, in which was hidden a small electric fuse and pyrotechnic ignitor card. The wire to fire this went up his sleeve, round the back and down to a switch which I held in my hand out of sight. So I was able to control the flash myself. This was another case of getting it in one take, for although we could have repeated the action, Paul Joyce, the Director, was happy. In a *Doctor Who* studio, it's all in a day's work …

ABOVE **A scene from 'Warriors of the Deep' in the TV studio. The Effects Department made both the Silurian heads and the working panels just visible on the bottom left.**

6
ON LOCATION

IT IS VERY unusual for *Doctor Who* not to go 'on location', but as I have already admitted, 'Warriors' Gate' was one of those exceptions to the rule! So I will use an earlier story to show how locations are handled – 'The Stones of Blood'.

The reason why *Doctor Who*, or any drama, goes on location is twofold. Firstly, there is never enough studio time for all the action, even in the five days. Secondly, locations can provide the sort of scenery it is hard to provide in a television studio.

What is a 'location' then? It is anywhere outside the TV studio; whether just down the street (though this is unlikely for *Doctor Who*) or hundreds of miles away. Usually what is wanted is something that is fairly non-Earth-like in appearance. The Earth is full of such places, but since they tend to be a long way away, *Doctor Who* locations are usually restricted to somewhere like a quarry, sand dunes or forests. There are exceptions, of course, and sometimes the Doctor will find himself visiting a stately home. There has also been the odd occasion when he has found himself abroad: he has turned up in Paris, Amsterdam and the Canary Islands, the last being used for their lunar-like landscape. Other out-of-the-ordinary locations have included Heathrow Airport and the Royal Festival Hall, and for 'The Stones of Blood', the Rollright Stones in Oxfordshire.

Going on location is like preparing for a studio, only worse. It is unlike a studio, where at least you can rush back to the workshop to do some major repair work or rebuilding. On location, which may be in the middle of nowhere, it is advisable to take absolutely everything with you. Stuck in the middle of a quarry, miles from the nearest shop is not the best time to realize you have not got any sticky tape! The weather on location is also unpredictable. It may well rain most of the time, so it is useful to have some sort of shelter around that can serve to keep everything, including yourselves, out of the elements.

Usually this will be the Visual Effects van which we use to transport all the gear, though we have to ensure that enough room is left for a portable workshop on board.

In general, effects on location are similar to those in the studio, except that they can be larger. An explosion that has to be done with Woofers and dropping boxes in the studio, can be done on a much larger scale outside. Large-scale weather effects, such as rain and wind, also come into their own on location, where full advantage can be taken of the surroundings. Special effects props though are no different; a radio communicator is a communicator wherever it is. Locations can however be a little more tiresome for the more delicate objects. Carefully clutching a fragile effects item while tripping over boulders or tree roots – or both – you soon begin to wonder why this particular sequence could not have been filmed in the middle of a high street!

For 'The Stones of Blood', the biggest items from an effects point of view were the Stones themselves. The Stones of the title were actually creatures called Ogri which spent most of their time in this rather frozen posture, disguised as stones. They lived for a great part of their time as part of a stone circle, hence the choice of the Rollright Stones as a location.

The Rollrights (the furthest south east of any stone circle in the British Isles) had the obvious advantage of being relatively close to London compared with other stone circles, and right next to a minor road which made access straightforward – some stone circles are miles off the beaten track. But even though the Rollrights are impressive, we had to add to them and make them even more so. This task was the responsibility of the Scenic Designer, John Stout, and myself. John provided some additional stones made out of expanded polystyrene (the same material as that used for ceiling tiles), while I had three 'real' Ogri made out of fibreglass. At the time I had working with me an Assistant, Roger Perkins, who had specialised in fibreglass work and moulding, so it took him a very short time to come up with three large fibreglass stone 'Ogri' all of which differed slightly, though I doubt if anyone noticed this subtlety.

RIGHT **A scene from 'K-9 and Company', shot on location at night, of a coven of witches about to make a sacrifice. The flaming torches called Flambeaux, are specially prepared.**

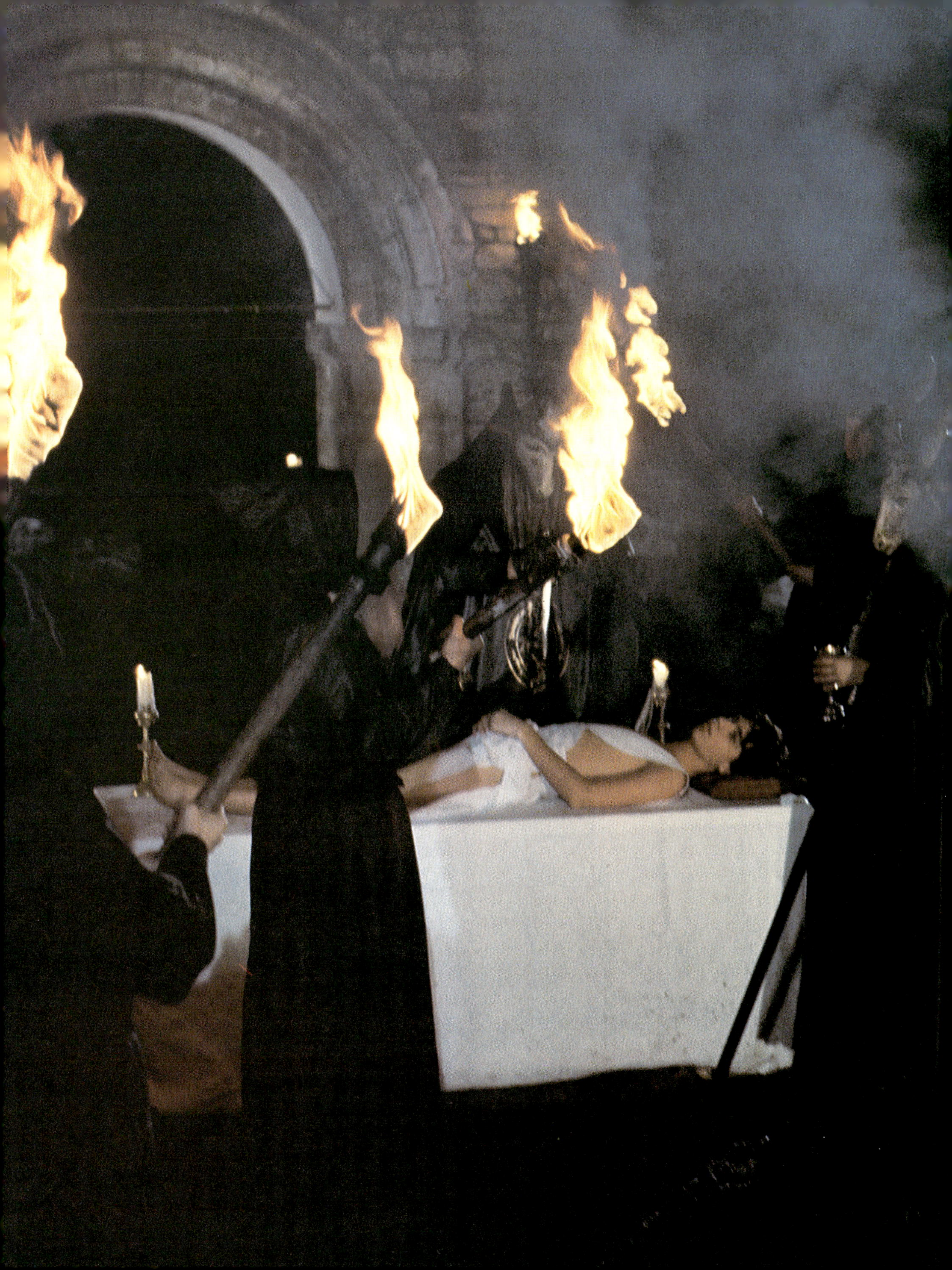

The Ogri had to move around at several times in the story and at this point of the original discussion with the Director, Darrol Blake, we could not decide whether or not to use actors in specially built rubber suits for these scenes. We eventually decided against this and I think we were right to stay with the solid stone form. Creatures of all sorts are probably the most difficult side of a *Doctor Who* story, and the Ogri were no exception. I think it would have been extremely difficult to use actors in 'monster' suits to look convincing as Ogri, and using completely solid shapes that merely glided around was a far better compromise. But this gliding around did cause problems, for how we were to levitate the stones without a lot of extra effects equipment? Overall I cheated, and you never saw the lower part of the Ogri while they moved. This was because each one was sitting on a trolley, and being pulled and pushed on ropes and pulleys by the Visual Effects Assistants. I suppose, thinking back on it, we could have hired cranes and flown the stones on wires, but although this sounds ideal, it is very expensive and time-consuming, and *Doctor Who* is short of both money and time. So it was down to the trolleys, which worked very well.

Wooden tracks were constructed in the workshop from thick blockboard, and they were designed to fit and bolt together

ABOVE **K-9 is manoeuvred into a suitable pose amongst the real Rollright Stones. In the background a fibreglass stone. The Ogri will be pulled along on a trolley to create movement.**

fairly easily. Side runners kept the trolley 'on the rails', and the trolleys themselves were fitted with large, plastic-wheeled castors and were relatively silent. The tracks were all straight, for although I contemplated a curved section, there was no point in going overboard with the idea! You don't need to see that much of a monster or creature for it to work successfully, really the less seen the better. (The cinema film *Alien* is a classic example of this.) The Ogri just moved silently for short periods at a time, seen in glimpses as they moved past trees, walls and gateways. How they moved was not important, just the fact they did, transferring from place to place. We did add one feature to the Ogri to make them different from the rest of the stones. As they were fibreglass they were also translucent, so each was fitted with lights inside, so they would glow eerily.

At one stage the fact they were equipped with lights caused a problem. One of the Ogri had to be lured to a cliff-top edge and tipped over. Would the lights ever survive the fall? The cliff was meant to be overlooking the sea; in reality it was a small quarry a couple of miles from the Rollrights, with about a seven-metre drop. The Ogri was positioned on its tracks, lights blazing, and pulled slowly towards the edge. Tipping the stone was achieved by the simple device of not bolting the Ogri down to the trolley, and stopping the latter suddenly. So that you would not see it, the electric lead that powered the lamps pulled itself free as the Ogri fell. The fact that the lamps went out at this stage was accepted as being perfectly natural for an Ogri and they were deemed expendable. In fact they miraculously survived the fall.

The trolleys that moved the Ogri also came in useful for another effect. This was still the era of K-9, and although he is reasonably fast on a flat surface, for a mechanical dog that is, get him anywhere near a bumpy surface and he could be overtaken by any tortoise in reasonable condition. One scene in 'The Stones of Blood' required K-9 to hurtle up the side of a field, do a right-angled turn and hurtle off into the distance at a far greater pace. Even if he had been fitted with a go-kart engine on a four-wheel-drive chassis he would have had a bit of a problem. So we had a dilemma.

In the end the problem was solved by attaching a length of thick fishing nylon to his front end to assist him along the first part of the run. At the point when he stopped at the corner, uttered some lucid K-9 remark, and then turned, he was helped by a second thick nylon line, to be pulled onto the Ogri trolley. This was hidden behind a low hedge and so the scene showed K-9 apparently taking off at a turn of speed never seen before – or since. It took five of us to do this one sequence – one on each nylon line, one on the radio control, one on the trolley rope and one flat on his back behind the hedge heaving K-9 onto the trolley and hoping he would not get run over!

Being on location does have its compensations, even if you don't appreciate it at the time. It's even sunny and hot sometimes! Eating your meals sitting in the sunshine does make a change from a dark TV studio, and there are some funny moments. It was on such a meal-break during 'The Stones of Blood' that a party of schoolchildren and their teacher turned up. As we were still occupied with eating, we said they could look around. It was some moments before we realized that they were counting the stones. And they were counting the polystyrene ones and the fibreglass one as well! What makes this even more ironic is that there is a legend associated with the Rollright Stones which says you can never accurately count them! It was not until they got all the way round that they were told they had counted the fake ones as well, which all goes to prove they must have looked fairly realistic.

BELOW **Visual Effects arrange a fitting end for the stone-like Ogri. The fibreglass creature has been pulled very fast on a trolley towards the cliff edge and allowed to tip naturally.**

7
MODELS AND MINIATURES

MODELS, OR MINIATURES, are the one aspect of Visual Effects that are literally in a world of their own. Where any special prop or floor effect is done within the context of the overall story, *Doctor Who* or anything else, the model filming can be taken out and regarded as being separate. Although models are always associated with science fiction and spaceships, and despite the fact *Doctor Who* model filming is largely taken up with them, models do extend over a far wider field.

The first read-through of a new script gives some idea of what model filming there is, if any. There may be mention of 'the Tardis flying through space and encountering another spaceship'. This immediately supposes there will be some models needed, but then 'a barren alien landscape' may be more easily created with a model landscape than with a full-sized one in the studio or on some far-flung location that will only roughly match.

This was the case on the first *Doctor Who* I ever did as a Visual Effects Designer, 'The Face of Evil'. The Doctor had climbed up a cliff face, and was looking out from a cave mouth across a vast plain. Sitting in the middle distance was a tall spaceship, almost like a tower. The scene was only ever viewed from this one place, and as it would have been impossible to build a full-sized set in the studio, or for that matter to find a suitable location that was not in the middle of a desert, this was a prime case for producing a miniature landscape. It was also a good example of a miniature that did not need to be very complicated. The 'landscape' was a single sheet of blockboard, with a few tiny details, such as rocks and bushes. The spaceship model, standing about 35 cms high, was built from construction kit parts, and supplied with a few low-voltage lights to illuminate the interior. The final setting of the scene was done with lighting, lamps on a white cyc, to produce an eerie orange glow in the sky.

Whatever the model needed for *Doctor Who*, it has to be built, and the construction of miniature spacecraft models has become an art in its own right. Not all models are built in the same way, however. There are many types of model-makers and all work in particular ways to produce different types of results. An architectural model-maker will not necessarily work in the same way as an exhibition model-maker, who will in turn have different priorities to a prototype model-maker, or a model enthusiast at home. Probably none of them will work quite like a special effects model-maker.

When it comes to constructing a special effects miniature, certain factors have to be borne in mind. This model will have to be handled and used, so it will have to be strong. Certain features such as lights and motors may have to work; and parts may have to move – landing gear may have to retract, for instance. The model will more than likely have to be supported at some stage of the filming process, so a suitable mount or mounts have to be built in. Rocket engines may have to work, which means using particular materials so that the whole model does not catch fire. If the model uses air jets for engines, pipes and tubes will have to be built in, and possibly made removable, in case they are visible in some shots. All this makes a special effects model different from other models, and when I am asked, as I often have been, 'What do you build the models out of?' I invariably reply, 'Anything and everything!' However, having said that, the most common material these days is probably plastic – in all its forms. But metal and wood still find their way into many a construction.

Returning to the *Doctor Who* I have been using as my main example, 'Warriors' Gate', the spaceship in this story was the Privateer. It forms as good an example as any of the whys and wherefores of special effects model-making.

The Privateer featured prominently in all the episodes of the

ABOVE RIGHT **The rocket for 'State of Decay' set up in the TV studio. It is on rostra to bring it to a suitable height for the two cameras in the foreground.**

BELOW RIGHT **Billowing out clouds of smoke, the Privateer spaceship from 'Warriors' Gate' lifts off. The glowing engines are created by Quartz Iodine bulbs and tiny fans built into the model.**

44

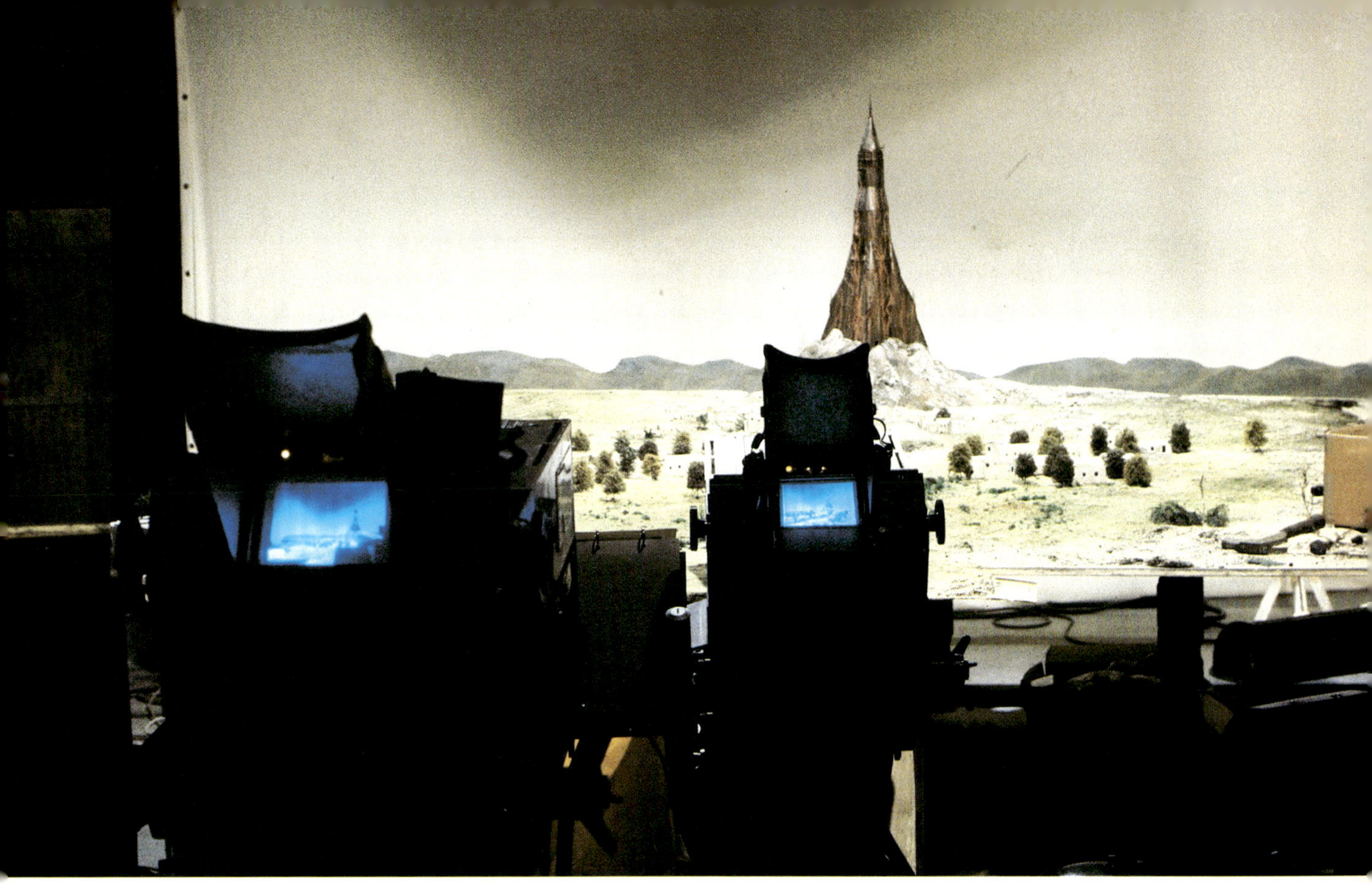

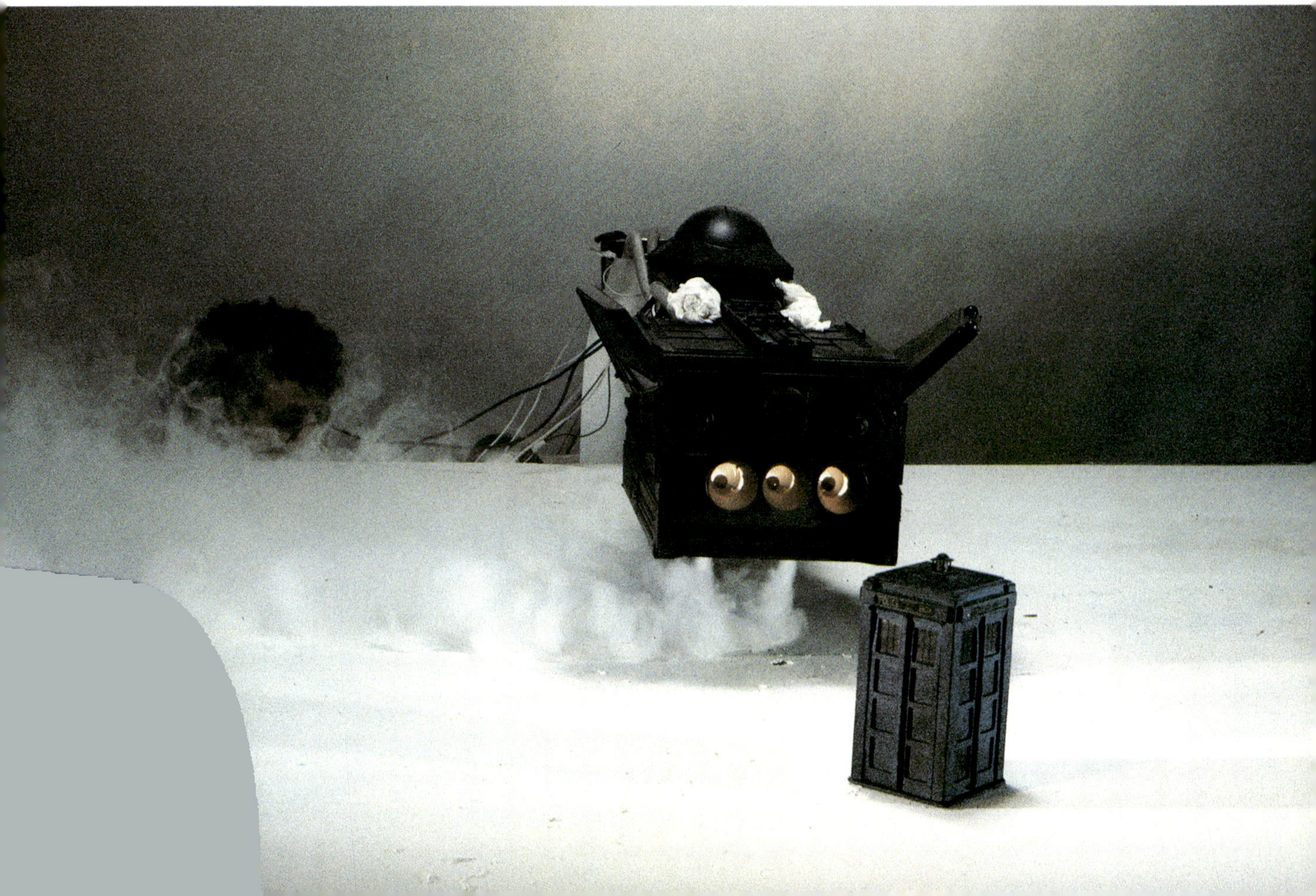

story and bowed out during the last minutes by exploding, having already demolished the Gate. When I read this, I immediately decided that, whatever else was required, I was going to need at the very least two models of the Privateer – one to blow up and one to do everything else. The all-important reason for this was that we wanted to be left with a skeletal framework of the Privateer after the explosion and fire. This meant building a special model for this one sequence which would not be suitable for the rest of the filming. A model that is going to have to explode is not going to be all that strong, and would not be suitable for what the Privateer was meant to do during the rest of the story.

The main model of the Privateer was therefore based around a strong metal frame which could be used to support the model in any orientation. Round this was built a plywood sheet covered with plastic sheeting. The final work was the dressing or detailing on this plastic with more plastic parts. This is where the art of using parts from commerical plastic kits and re-adapting them to another purpose comes into its own. This

BELOW **This wrecked version of the Privateer was specially constructed so that when it was blown up the main body, made from thin plastic, would melt but the skeleton framework would be left behind.**

ABOVE **The two models of the Privateer side by side. The metal framework of the one on the left was later covered in plastic sheet to match the 'real' Privateer on the right.**

is invariably known as 'kit-bashing'. The interesting point here is that the kit you use does not necessarily *have* to be a model of a spaceship. Any type of model kit can be used, from aircraft to ships, tanks and even railway buildings. Many an Airfix girder bridge kit has found its way into a spaceship model. There are also special parts manufacturers, the best known of which is Engineering Model Associates (EMA), who produce a vast range of plastic parts originally for commercial petro-chemical plant model-makers, but who the effects model-makers soon discovered and took over in force.

I think I was probably one of the first (if not the first) in this country to use EMA parts for effects models. When I first visited their shop way back in 1970, their window was full of model oil refineries and petro-chemical plants. These days it's full of weird and wonderful spaceships!

From the script, and working with the Scenic Designer, Graeme Story, we knew that the Privateer had to have certain features that would fit in with the story. There was an air-lock that had to be at ground level as it was featured in a number of scenes. The bridge was fairly high up, and at the back were several largish engines. There was some damage at ground level which was represented by a small hole in the model (and a fairly large hole in Graeme's set!). Otherwise, the design was up to me. Lights were not specified either, but I added two powerful headlamps from Quartz Iodine (QI) bulbs. These are small, but very powerful, and consequently very hot. We had to be very careful not to leave them on too long or they would melt their surroundings.

The engines also had to glow, and this too came from QI bulbs, with the addition of some smoke blown out by three small electric motors running model boat propellers as fans. Some other small lamps were also added, from model railway signals, to give some detail in a couple of areas.

Meanwhile, we were building the Privateer that was going to explode. I did most of the work on the 'proper' Privateer model (though Designers do not normally do any of the actual manufacturing), while one of my Assistants, Steve Lucas (now also a Visual Effects Designer) made the exploding model. He built up a skeleton of thick wire to match the overall shape of the model I was building. It did not have to match exactly as there was no occasion when they would be directly compared. Inside he added a lot of cross-bracing and struts which were not on my model. These were to make the final burnt-out model look as if it originally had some internal structure. He salvaged some largish metal items that would not burn from the bits and pieces bin to add internal detail. The engine remains were, for example, the volume controls of an old radio set and metal cigar tubes.

On the outside, Steve clad the model with thin plastic sheet, and added a certain amount of the detailing I was adding to my model. Again this did not have to match exactly as it would only be seen in this state for a split second before it blew up. Room was left at the back to pack the insides with pyrotechnics when we actually got to the model filming.

The Privateer was not the only model in the programme. It was also decided to make the Gate as a model, because not only had it to be demolished at the end, but the design that had been chosen would anyway have been too large for the studio. As it was, the Gate came in two parts: the doorway, which was built full-size and which stood at the front, and a tall cathedral-like window which stretched up behind the gateway.

Knowing the model was going to have to be exploded also dictated the way it was built. To construct a building, as against a craft, usually means employing different techniques. As we presumed that the gate and window were built of some sort of 'brick' type material (though this is not necessarily so in a science fiction story), the two items were moulded from plaster. This meant making a mould first, because although I was only building one Privateer to explode, the Gate if anything was more important and since we could not guarantee to get the scene right first time I decided we should make two of each part. We also decided to make a smaller version of the gate which would fit in with the white landscape of the 'nothing' far better in relationship to the model Tardis and the Privateer.

Having made these decisions, the next task was to model up the original of the gate and window out of clay. Once completed, a fibreglass mould was taken of this, and when hardened, the clay scraped out. This left what is called a female mould, into which we poured Plaster of Paris. This dries very quickly, and in no time at all the finished gate and window could be carefully eased out of the mould. It is best to make these kinds of moulds in several pieces and then bolt them together. Then, by undoing the bolts and pulling the mould away one piece at a time, the model comes out much easier than if the mould was in one piece. One of my Assistants at the time, Bryony Keating, spent many days making these models, and

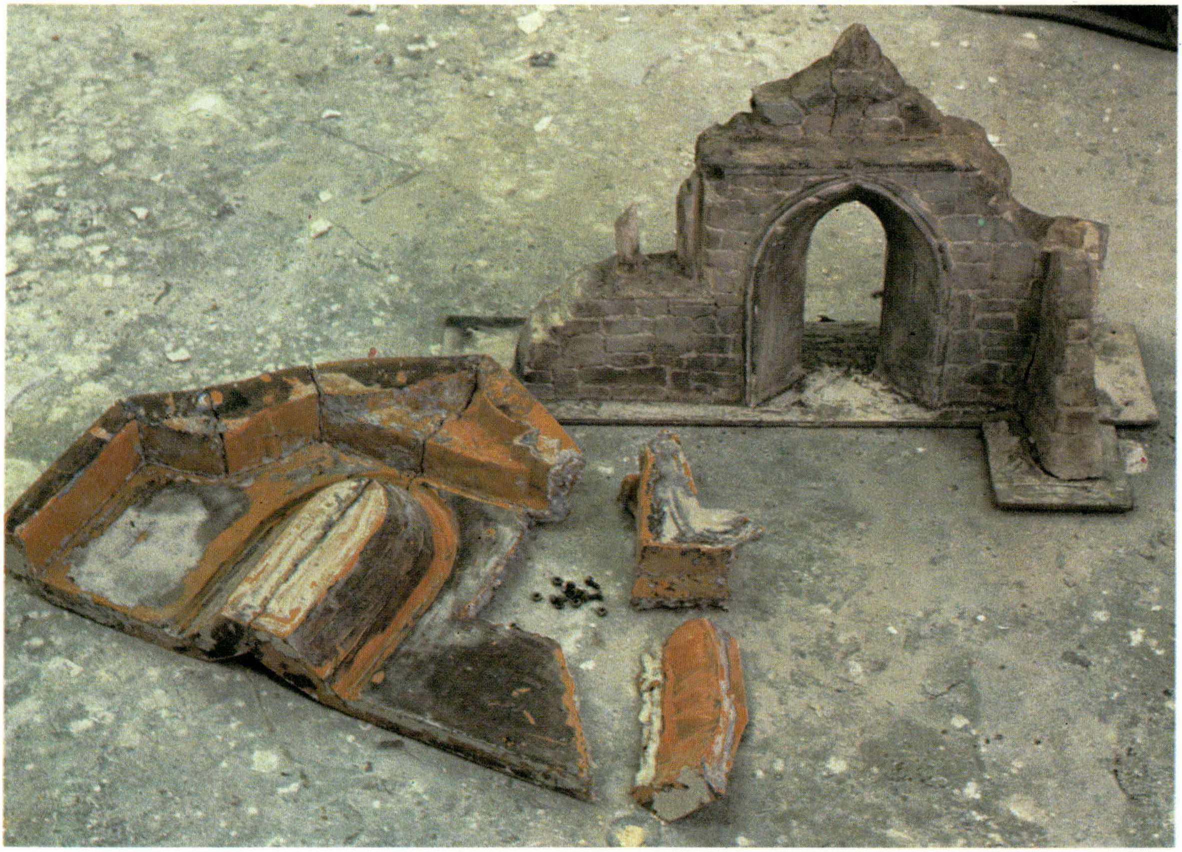

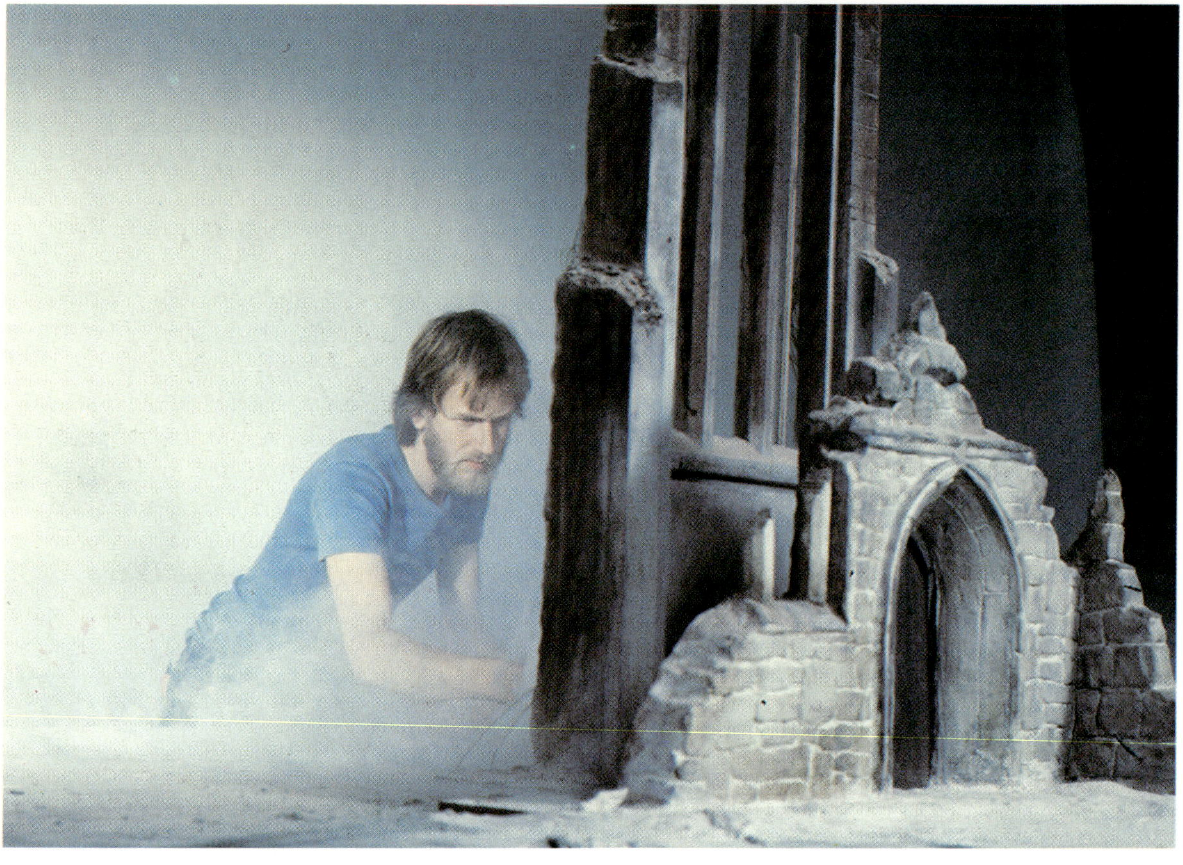

ABOVE LEFT **The gateway from 'Warriors' Gate' was built in miniature out of plaster. This was poured into the fibreglass mould in the foreground which is then split into several parts to release the cast.**

BELOW LEFT **Steve Lucas begins to wire up the pyrotechnic charges behind the Warriors' Gate gateway which will soon blow the model to pieces. In all, twenty separate charges were used.**

then painting them. Plaster luckily takes water-based colours very well. The Gate was to be in palish colours, with the foreground door reddish, and the window pale blue. A thin wash of these colours was applied to the plaster, and it soaked into the surface. Adding more paint gradually built up the colour, and fine details and shading were applied with a brush.

With the models well on their way to being completed, I was able to turn my attention to the actual model filming. At this stage though I should point out a few things about the difference between film cameras and the electronic versions.

I think that it is fairly well known that there are two ways to produce a moving picture on a screen. You can either use photographic film or you can electronically record the picture on videotape. Film was the original way of producing a picture, and so we had cinema films long before television. Film is of course still used a great deal, both by the cinema and by television. But videotape is being used more and more by television companies to produce pictures far quicker than from film. The obvious use is in news broadcasts where you can not only play back the recorded picture very quickly, but you can also 'insert' the pictures 'live' on air, which is the way television works anyway. This is something film cannot do. Even cinema film-makers are now using video to make 'films' and here the words used for each process do get somewhat jumbled up. Film terminology, because it is the older process, tends to be more widespread, and we say 'we are going filming', even if we are using video cameras. And the expression 'model filming' is used whether the models are being filmed with film cameras or video recorded with electronic cameras. Consequently, it can get a bit confusing.

You may wonder why we still use film when video seems to be so much better, but it is not quite as straightforward as that. The two types of picture definitely look different and many people, both those of us who make the programmes, and those who watch them, prefer the 'look' of film. Others, however, prefer the 'look' of the electronic video picture, though I'm not one of them. Film also has a great advantage when it comes to model filming and here it should reign supreme for some years.

To understand why we use film cameras almost exclusively when it comes to filming miniatures it is necessary to understand a little about how each camera works. The film camera has a reel of undeveloped film, each frame of which is really a single 'still' picture. The film runs at so many frames per second through the gate of the camera, and it is projected at the same speed. When it is projected you are actually seeing so many still pictures per second on the screen, but this speed is so fast that the brain is tricked into thinking they are moving. This is called persistence of vision.

Television also uses persistence of vision, but the pictures are built up electronically and scanned on to your television screen. For normal 'filming' both techniques are very similar, and both 'run' at more or less the same speed of 25 frames per second (fps). (Cinema films use 24 frames per second, television adds the extra frame for film for technical reasons). The 'frames' on the electronic image are not frames you can hold up to the light and see, like you can a cine film, but they still exist on the videotape.

Now, all this is fine for most images, but when it comes to filming miniatures there is a problem with the electronic way of filming. Because the models are smaller than they would be in real life, they do not move in a realistic manner. A miniature Lunar Buggy travelling across the Moon's surface will be rocking about in a far more violent way than if it was full-sized. The same can be said when moving spaceship models, or filming model explosions. It will all happen at a far greater speed than it would do if the spaceship, or the explosion, was done full-sized.

The answer is to slow down the movement, so that it appears slower. One way would be to slow down the film projector or videotape recorder, but in doing this, as there are only 25 pictures per second anyway, you soon begin to see a jerky sort of movement like an old-fashioned silent film. (This used to happen because they *did* run at the slower speed of 16 frames per second.) So, as you cannot slow down the finished film, you have to speed up the original film camera, which is precisely what is done. You can very easily run film cameras at far greater speeds than 25 fps, but you cannot normally do this with electronic cameras, although present research may allow us to do it in the future. This is one aspect of electronic research that is still being explored. So if I think that a model will be moving, or there is a fire or explosion, I have no choice – I have to use film. And of course, in 'Warriors' Gate', there were lots of fires and explosions.

With the construction of the Privateer and the Gate underway, and the Tardis model already available, the next stage was to build the miniature set. Like the full-size 'nothing' in the television studio, this 'nothing' also had to appear white overall. But I could not use the CSO method. The way of using coloured backgrounds on film to 'insert' another picture is called the Blue Screen Process and has been used in many cinema films like *Star Wars* and *ET*. But using this method takes a lot of time, which is something we do not have much of when making a *Doctor Who*. So we needed actually to colour the background white. Everyone then had to remember not to walk all over it! Of course, everyone did when setting up the models, so it had to be constantly repainted.

Moving models in a miniature set is always a problem. Luckily only the Privateer was going to have to move in this batch of filming. Even then it did not have to move very far or very fast. Most shots required it to have just lifted off, and possibly to turn slightly, before settling down again.

Before filming begins, all the model shots that are needed are drawn out in picture form, called a story board because it 'tells the story' of these particular sequences. In fact in a large feature film the whole film is 'storyboarded', so everyone has some idea of what is going on. These drawings need not be anything elaborate, just a quick sketch, although sometimes a more elaborate drawing in colour is better. Occasionally one stage further is needed and a model of the model will be made, in a very rough form, to get some idea of what the finished model

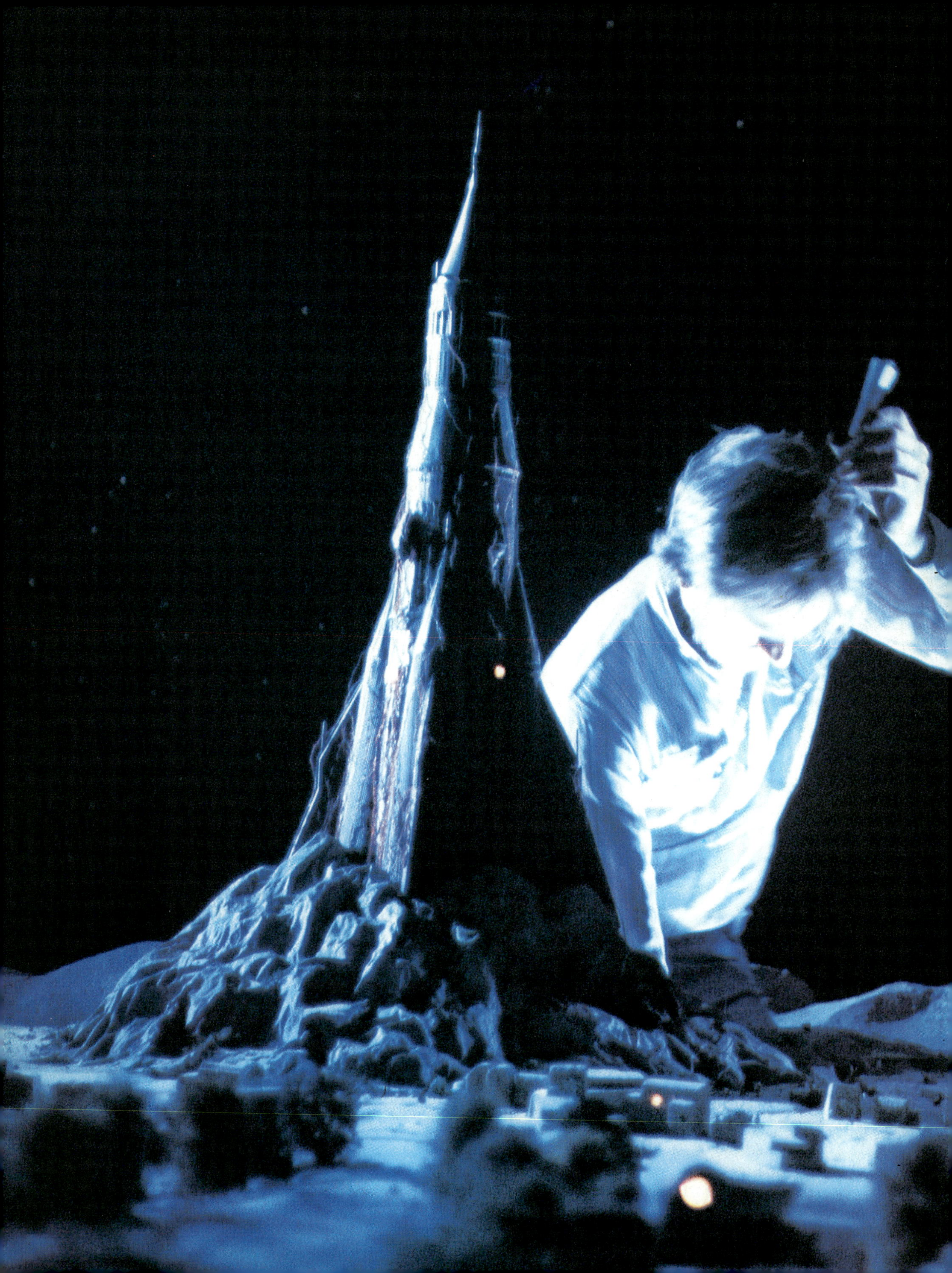

A miniature scene is built for the story 'State of Decay'. The tower in the background, a space rocket in disguise, has been sculpted from polystyrene and detailed with small plastic parts. The tiny village below the tower was built in a similar way with added touches such as trees and bushes.
Chris Lawson and Tony Harding are wiring up a small pyrotechnic explosion on the tower where a model missile will strike.

will be like. For although two-dimensional drawings can get across many of the ideas, they are no substitute for an object that can be picked up and viewed from any angle. 'Warriors' Gate' did not have models made 'of the models', but for 'Warriors of the Deep', small replicas were made of both the creature and the underwater base before the larger versions were made. Armed with the storyboard, I, as Effects Designer, can then discuss the shots with the Director to make sure that what I intend to film will fit in with his action. Normally the Effects Designer will direct his own model film sequence as the actual Director is invariably tied up rehearsing. This obviously involves quite a bit of discussion with the film cameraman.

Model filming, unlike a television studio, involves very few people. There is no sound, for example, since model filming is always shot 'mute'. Again, because the sets are small, compared to a full-size set, not all that many lights are needed and this reduces the number of people. All in all, most model shots can take place with no more than six people.

For 'Warriors' Gate', I discussed the shots with the cameraman, and decided on their order. Some of this order was more logical than others. For example, the final explosion would destroy the Gate and so there would be no sense in doing this shot at the beginning! Other shots are what are called 'establishers' and put the scene into perspective. Normally you do not film a shot that is completely static. There should always be some movement. Either something in the scene moves, or alternatively, the camera moves around the shot. Sometimes, though, you just need briefly to 'see the scene outside', to make sure it is still there, in which case a non-moving shot can just about be tolerated. As far as this was concerned, the 'Warriors' Gate' model scenes were not the easiest to plan as the only object that would do any moving as such, and then only a few times, was the Privateer. Once the Tardis had arrived it stayed put until right at the end, when it disappeared, and of course the Gate did not move until right at the end, when it did so rather violently. So all movement was down to the Privateer. It was a large craft in 'full-size', so would move in a rather lumbering fashion. For the take-off and landing shots the movement was done by an air-ram that pushed an arm up and down. The Privateer was fixed on the end of the arm. The engines that supposedly lifted the craft would produce a lot of smoke, so pipes to provide smoke were fixed along this arm and disappeared down into the main body of the model. The cables to supply current to all the lights also went down this arm.

So the Privateer could now get off the ground, but it also had to turn, and here I used a different method. Some time before, I had done the model filming for the pilot programme of the series *QED*, about human error. One sequence required the crashing of two aircraft, which does tend to be a bit expensive, so we used models instead. In the lead-up to the crash, the aircraft needed to be seen to taxi and turn on the runways, and to get them to move in a realistic fashion I borrowed some small turntables from our film department. They are actually designed to display items, like vases borrowed from museums, so that the camera can film all the way round, without having actually to move all the way round. The movement is very precise and when I sat the model aircraft on this turntable it turned round – or looked as if it was turning round – just like a full-size aircraft. So when it came to moving the Privateer, I remembered these turntables and borrowed one again. By sitting the model on the turntable, adjusting the speed and by positioning the camera so that it was looking up at the craft, the whole bulk of the model would seem to swing round past the camera, as if the ship was heaving herself round.

The final sequence for the story was the blowing up of both the Privateer and the Gate. The 'real' Privateer model was changed for the 'skeleton' version, and the Gate and the ship wired up with miniature pyrotechnic devices. In all about twenty were used, sixteen on the Gate, which would explode first, and the remaining ones on the Privateer. To fire all these in sequence, I used a rotary switch, which fired one charge at a time. The filming speed was very important for this sequence, as a miniature explosion does not know that it is 'miniature' and will go off at the same speed as if it was 'full-size'. So this really is a time for 'high-speed' model filming. Remembering that the normal speed for a television film camera is 25 fps, I had been filming most of the shots at 75 fps, which by a quick bit of arithmetic you can see is three times the normal speed. This means that by the time the film is projected at the normal 25 fps, all the movement has slowed down to a third of its actual speed, so the lumbering movement of the Privateer would become even more lumbering. But for the explosion, 75 fps would not be anything like fast enough. I had to shoot this at 500 fps, which is twenty times faster than normal. There are not many cameras that can go at this sort of speed, but one that can is called a Locam. (It has a companion which goes even faster and is called, perhaps not surprisingly, a Hycam!)

I also decided to use not one, but two film cameras on this shot, and to do the sequence again, so that I would end up with four pieces of film. The second camera, which I had already been using, was a Mitchell camera that used 35 millimetre film. There are various film standards, and 35 mm is *the* standard. (This was the size used for most cinema films, although these days they use the wider 70 mm film especially for wide-screen spectaculars.) Half the size of 35 mm is 16 mm which is the film size used most for television. The Locam uses 16 mm, so I had two cameras using two different sizes of film for the shots. The 35 mm Mitchell camera will not run as fast as the Locam; 120 fps is its maximum, so it was positioned closer in to take close-

ABOVE **The end of the gateway. The first two pictures show the wooden door at the base blowing out, while later in the sequence carefully placed charges destroy the arched window.**

up detail of the Gate. The Locam was set further back, to photograph the whole scene.

With the cameras in position, the pyrotechnics were wired up and everyone donned a safety helmet and goggles. The model stage-doors were shut and guarded to prevent anyone suddenly strolling in, and the last-minute checks were made. Then both cameras were switched on, and checked to ensure they were running at the correct speed before the camera operators retreated to safety. Then I started the rotary switch and all the charges began to go off. Bits of gateway flew all over the place, and then the Privateer started to explode as well. It seemed an age but in reality it was all over in about twelve seconds. But of course the high-speed cameras made sure that there would be very much more than twelve seconds-worth of final film – more like over two minutes. With this first sequence done, the baseboard was cleared and the second Gate set up to repeat the shot. Because there was not a second Privateer, this shot was only of the Gate. Again both cameras were used, and again all the safety checks gone through before the cameras began to roll. Once again bits of Gate flew all over the model stage.

There were then only two things left to do. Firstly, clear the chaos. Secondly, wait until the next day to see the 'rushes' (the first prints of the film) to see whether it had all worked. Luckily that time it did.

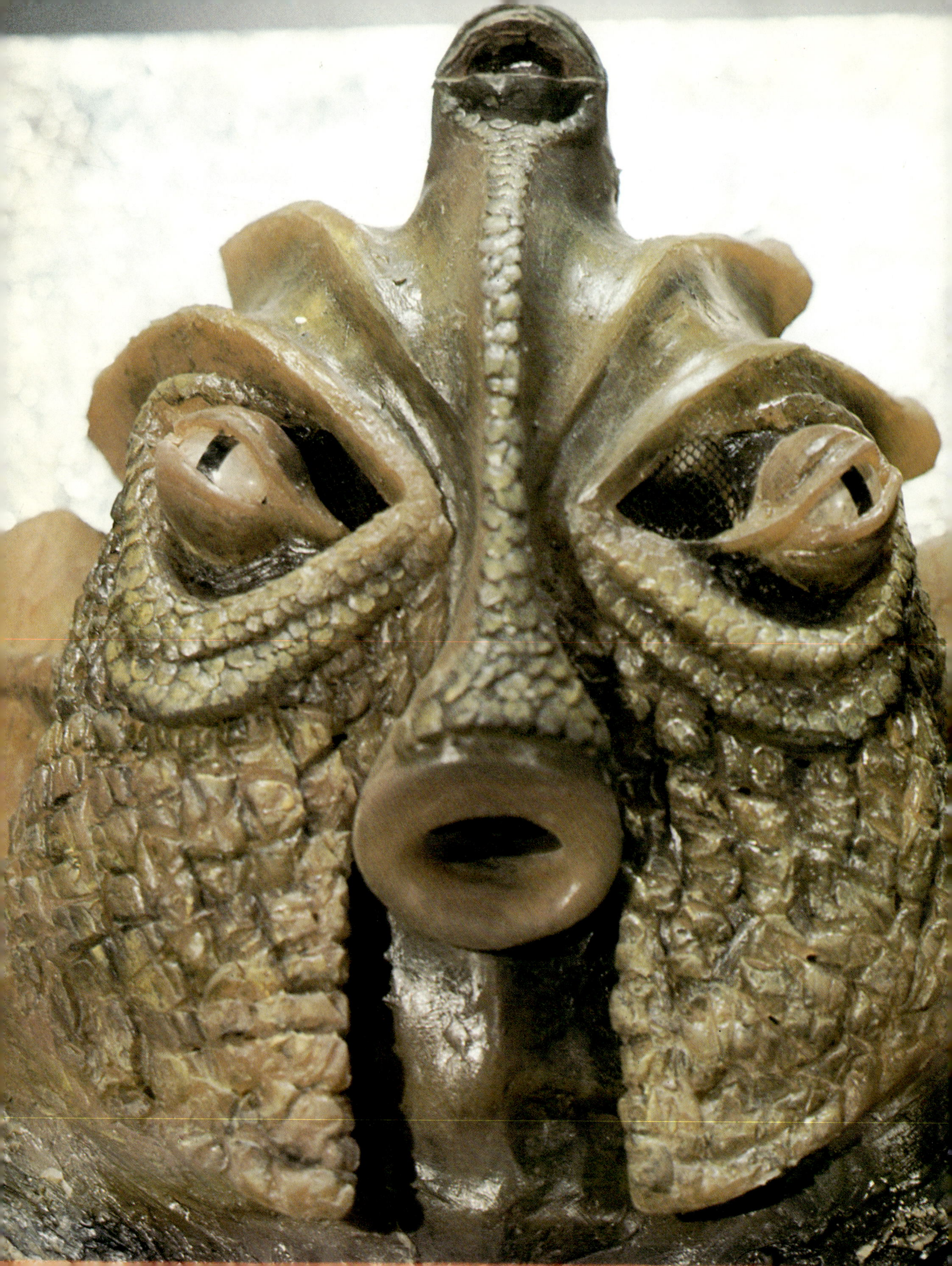

8
MONSTERS AND CREATURES

I CAN'T SAY I'm too fond of monsters. Some work better than others, but there is also the question of when is a monster not a monster? The answer is: when it's an effect, and a lot of *Doctor Who* monsters end up as effects. The term 'monster' is not really quite right when applied to this programme, for there are many so-called 'monsters' that are perfectly benevolent aliens. And what about the robots? Perhaps the better overall term is 'creature', which includes all non-human participants.

Some are more famous – or should it be infamous – than others, and the most infamous of the lot, the Daleks, have their own chapter. But there have been many others during the lifetime of the series, some of which make re-appearances from time to time and others which are seen but briefly and then disappear into the mists of time.

For any proposed creature in a *Doctor Who* story, the Effects Designer, the Costume Designer and the Make-Up Designer will have to get into a huddle, because most *Doctor Who* creatures actually have somebody inside them. The dividing-line between whether a creature is an Effect or a Costume is very thin and usually nonexistent. Broadly speaking if it is a 'solid' costume, it is an effect, and if it is a 'flexible' costume, it is a costume. It is in fact usually a combination of both – Effects will make sections of a creature's skin, which Costume will then stitch and glue together as the costume. The Draconians from the story 'The Frontier in Space' are a good example here, with layers and layers of Draconian scales being prepared in the Effects workshop out of latex, and then passed over to the Costume department, for cutting up and assembling. Masks are treated similarly. The skin texture may very well have to match the body, like the Draconians again, but the mask will

LEFT **The original version of the Silurian. The shape was first sculpted in clay, then a plaster mould taken. Next latex was poured into the mould and, when cured, pulled free. Careful painting created the final result.**

have to be finally fitted to the actors by the Make-Up department, and areas around the eyes, mouth and nose blended in with the actors' own.

The Cybermen, second only to the Daleks in infamy, have always been a combined effort, with Costume providing the basic costume for the actor, and Effects providing such items as the life-support systems. Sometimes the division of labour is not so cut and dried. In 'Warriors of the Deep', where there were two sets of creatures, the Silurians and the Sea Devils, Costume provided both sets of costumes and the masks for the Sea Devils, while Effects did the masks for the Silurians. There is no logic there at all, because, although produced by the Costume Department, two Sea Devils had to be modified by Effects – one Sea Devil was given operating radio-controlled eyelids, and a second was given the full 'death from asphixiation' treatment.

The materials that go into the making of a creature are as varied as the creatures themselves. Given that most of them are

ABOVE **Steve Drewett with his pet Hordas from 'The Face of Evil'. On the left is a radio-controlled version while Steve holds one with mechanical jaws and a lot of teeth.**

ABOVE LEFT **The head of Sutek for 'The Pyramids of Mars'. This was not fitted to the actor but operated by Effects people from behind.**

ABOVE RIGHT **Sutek, played by Gabriel Wolfe, wears a mask supposedly over the Sutek head though in reality it just covered the actor's face.**

going to be occupied by an actor, the main consideration the Designers – Effects and Costume – have is to make it as comfortable as possible for them, which is not always that easy.

The majority of creature costumes are made out of latex – or rubber – in one form or another, and latex can get extremely hot under studio conditions. Frankly, there is little that can be done about this, and the Designer will attempt to ensure that at least the mask is easily removable so that the actor can have a break during recording. I have to stick to latex because it is the one material that is easily mouldable and flexible, so it is ideal.

An original is modelled up, whether it be the mask of a creature, or a section of its skin, from clay. This is worked on until the Designer is satisfied that it will work as the creature. A plaster cast is then taken of the original, and when dry, the clay is removed. You then have a negative or female mould of the original rather like the early stages of building a model. If the final mask is to be made in latex, this can very simply be poured into the mould, swilled round and the excess poured out. A dry, warm place will cure the latex very quickly, and a second layer can then be poured in. It is a matter of judging how thick the mask should be made, as the more layers the heavier, but at the same time the more rigid. A balance has to be struck. Often supporting pieces cut from foam can be added which will keep the weight down, but still add rigidity. Eventually the finished mask can be pulled out of the mould and a second one started. The first will need finishing and painting but otherwise it is almost ready to use.

If the final mask is to be made from fibreglass, which is the other most popular material, this is a slightly different, and more tricky process. Fibreglass, unlike latex, is rigid, and will not come out of a mould that has any undercuts. Undercuts occur if the original sculpture had complicated areas where a material such as fibreglass would get stuck. So if the final mask is known to be in such a material, the original mould will have to be made in several pieces like the gateway in 'Warriors' Gate'. Fibreglass will also stick to plaster unless a release agent is used, so this is something else to bear in mind. If many fibreglass masks are to be taken it will probably be better to make the original mould from fibreglass as well.

Some smaller, less complicated masks can be made by a process called vacuum-forming where a thin plastic sheet is heated and stretched down over a mould. The air is removed from between them and the plastic takes on the shape of the mould. It is a very quick, and cheap, way of producing a wide variety of shapes. *Doctor Who* creatures that have employed such a procedure have included the robots from 'The Robots of Death', and the Gundans from 'Warriors' Gate'.

Some creatures are too small even to contemplate having someone inside them. K-9 is the most well-known here, and he too has his own chapter. Others are even smaller than K-9: the Cybermen's pet Cybermats, the Hordas from 'The Face of Evil', and the Spiders from 'The Planet of the Spiders'. All relied on mechanics rather than humans for movement, although humans were of course behind the 'remote' control. The spiders used a whole variety of techniques, both in

ABOVE **Boris revealed! The only fully mechanical spider model from 'Planet of the Spiders' seen in his true light – a collection of Meccano, gears, a chain, a motor and batteries.**

construction and in operation. Some were constructed using the mould and latex method, while others were quickly turned out courtesy of the vacuum-forming machine. Operational methods ranged from cables allowing the spider to be operated from underneath, to puppet-like wires and self-contained motorized versions. I was in fact personally responsible for building the prototype spider. It is a creation that has travelled with me ever since!

Boris was the only spider that was completely self-contained: no strings, no wires, nobody. Just a large, hairy spider that would scurry across the floor after Sarah Jane. My big problem was that the bulk of the spiders had already been constructed, and there was not time to start from scratch, I had to use one of the existing vacuum-formed bodies as a basis. My old friend, since departed back to the film world, Ian Scoones, had been turning these out. Each was then equipped with a set of legs, courtesy of Steve Bowman who spent days pouring latex into a 'leg' mould. Consequently, it was not a case of 'building a spider to fit a mechanism', rather 'building a mechanism to fit a spider'! I had honestly intended to construct a 'production' version after the prototype, but as usual time ran out and it was the prototype that appeared on the screen.

This spider was going to have to move like a real spider, but there was no way that the legs would carry the body. So the body had to be on wheels, and the leg movement was really incidental. It was then just a matter of laying out all the components: motors, gears and wheels, and seeing what was the smallest space you could actually fit them in. Most of the mechanism, the gears and wheels especially, was Meccano, which has proved very useful to the Visual Effects Department over the years.

Boris – and I am using his adopted name here as I cannot think of him by any other – eventually came together and a quick demonstration across the workshop floor showed he might even work! The body had had to be enlarged slightly to hide the 'rowing-boat' action legs, but otherwise I had used the original shape. Boris was not, as some have since suggested to me, radio-controlled, so once switched on, there was no way of switching him off, except by charging across the studio floor and doing a rugby tackle in an attempt to reach his switch before he piled into the scenery, legs flying everywhere. Boris is a *Doctor Who* creature I have decided I could live with, though I am not sure about some of the others.

BELOW **Boris more as he would have appeared in the series. The covering, a mixture of fake fur and broom hairs, was glued to rubber legs and a vacuum-formed plastic body.**

9
THE DALEKS

MOST NOTORIOUS OF all the *Doctor Who* creatures, and probably of all science fiction stories as well, are the Daleks. Most *Doctor Who* creatures have been influenced by the person operating them which has given them certain human characteristics. The Daleks have somehow managed to avoid this and the way they glide around, almost silently, coupled with their total lack of compassion, has made them creatures people love to hate.

Daleks are always called robots, though they are not in the true sense of the word. Rather they are an extension of a creature's body which became so withered and incapable of any movement that this external 'shell' – the Dalek – had to be constructed to allow the creature to survive. This original storyline is now lost, apart from in a couple of episodes.

The Daleks were the first *Doctor Who* creatures, and the script by Terry Nation described them in great detail. Ray Cusick (the Scenic Designer) who faithfully interpreted Terry Nation's script, described them as 'pepperpot shaped, silently moving' – apparently they were supposed to be similar to Georgian State Dancers gliding across the floor! The design was the combined efforts of Terry Nation, Ray Cusick, Jack Kine, Bernard Wilkie and the contractors who assembled the first Daleks.

It is hard to believe that Daleks do have people working them from inside! An operator sits on a tiny bench, and pushes the creature around with his feet. In front are the two controls for the gun and the sink plunger, and overhead is a handle to swivel the head. A switch operates the lights, but the operators do not do the Dalek voices, which come from off-stage.

The earliest Daleks were constructed from wood. Fibreglass was then used to form the top dome, which is actually not a true dome, a wire grill was fixed around the centre, and small

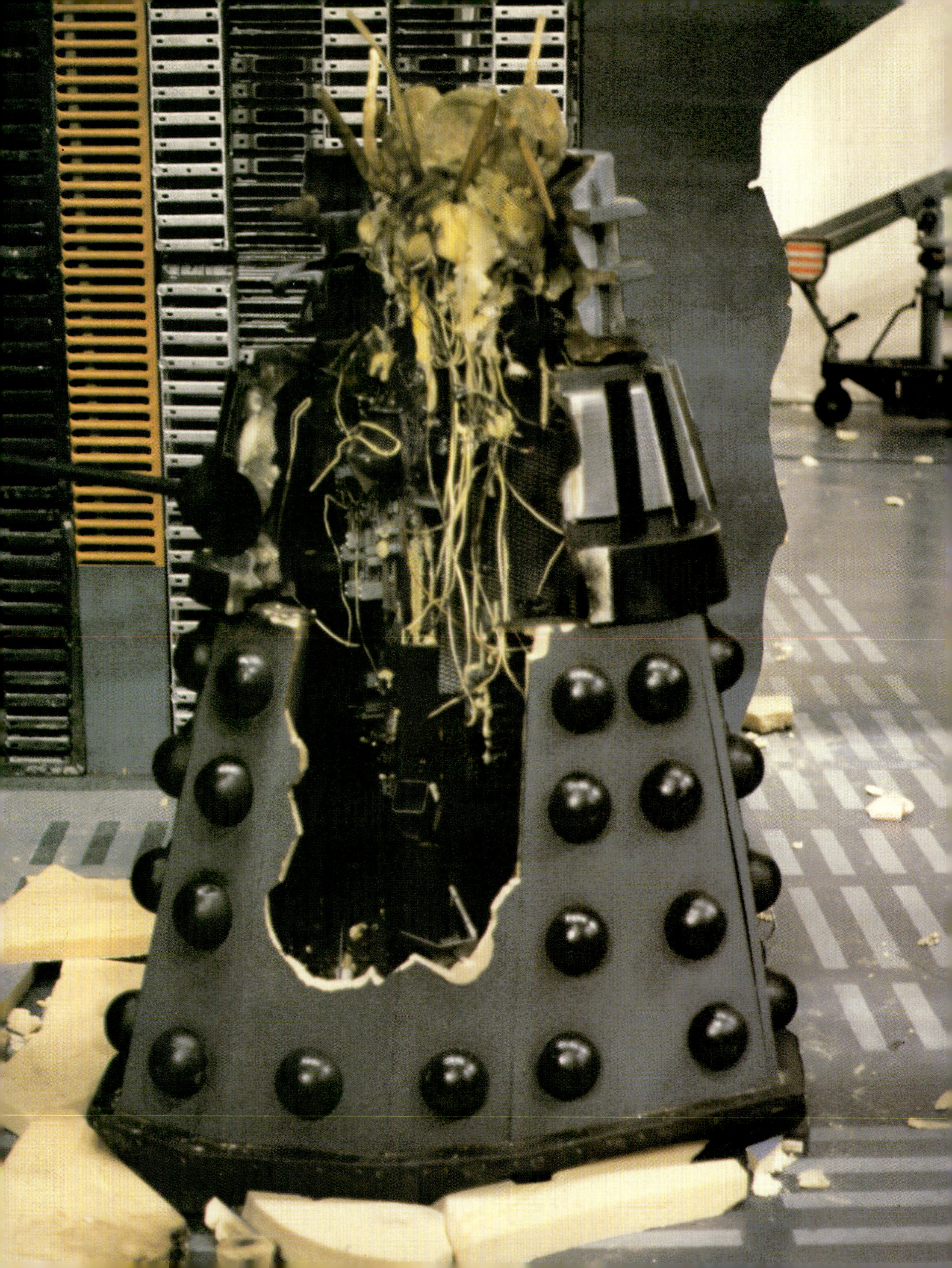

LEFT **Daleks that move around have an actor inside them but when they need to be destroyed, they are replaced with versions specially built from lightweight, breakable materials.**

hemispheres added around the body. The whole thing was then mounted on castors – and there was a Dalek.

There have never been all that many Daleks. Over the years the BBC has probably had no more than a dozen at various times. More were made for the cinema film, but these were never used for the TV series. In recent years no more than four were ever available, and when new stories were written featuring the Daleks, more had to be built. Fibreglass was used to a greater extent in these later versions, but otherwise the pattern was very much the same as twenty years ago.

Daleks turned up in a variety of colours which may or may not have signified some sort of rank. Chief Daleks tended to be black and gold, though this varied, and others were various shades. Whatever their colour, Daleks have always been the same overall shape, with two notable exceptions: the Emperor Dalek in the story 'The Evil of the Daleks', a static, spherical creature, and then Davros, who created the Daleks in the first place and who featured in the story 'Genesis of the Daleks'. The story was written to answer some of the questions about the Daleks' origin, and it gave the opportunity to extend the way the Daleks operated.

The actor playing Davros sat in the same way as the operator, in a base that matched the base of the Daleks. Switches allowed Davros to keep control over everything and the final touch was a newly-created Davros mask. The original version was designed and made by John Friedlander. It was sculpted in clay, a plaster mould made, and then a mask was taken in latex. For recordings, the mask was fitted to the actor and blended in by the Make-up Designers. Metal wires and fitting, including Davros's third eye, were built in to the mask as it was constructed, and gloves were covered with suitable Davros 'skin'.

Davros reappeared in a more recent story 'Resurrection of the Daleks', but it was discovered that the original Davros mask had dried out and cracked too badly to be saved. As the original mould had also long gone, a new version was sculpted, this time by Stan Mitchell, which kept the spirit of the original,

DALEK · DRAWING Nº 1
GENERAL DETAIL MARK 4. MODEL

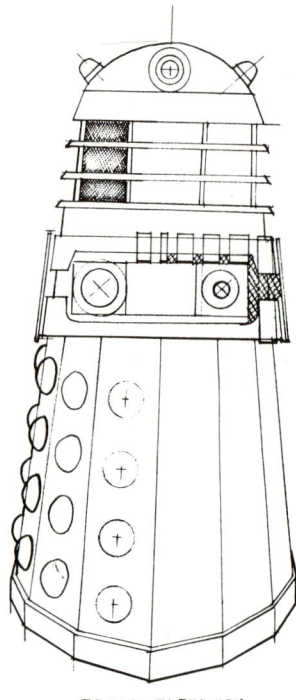

FRONT ELEVATION.

SCALE

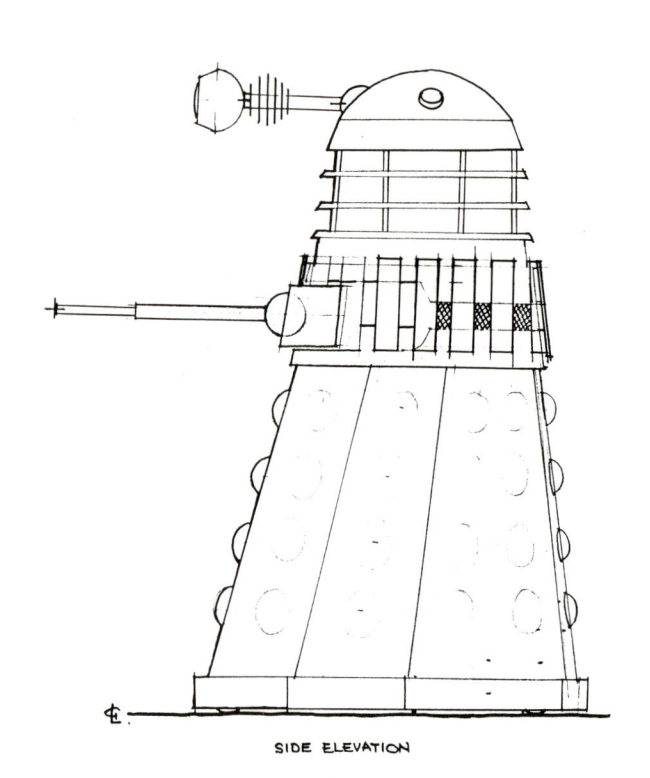

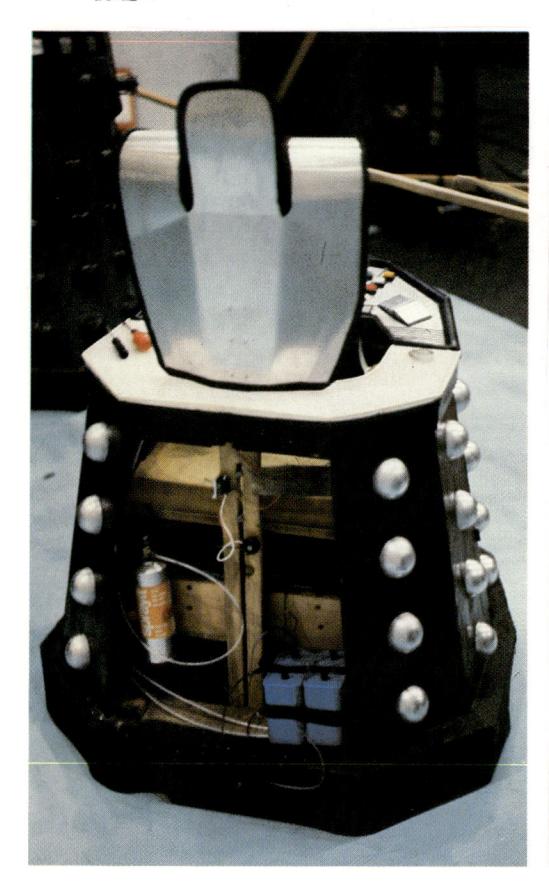

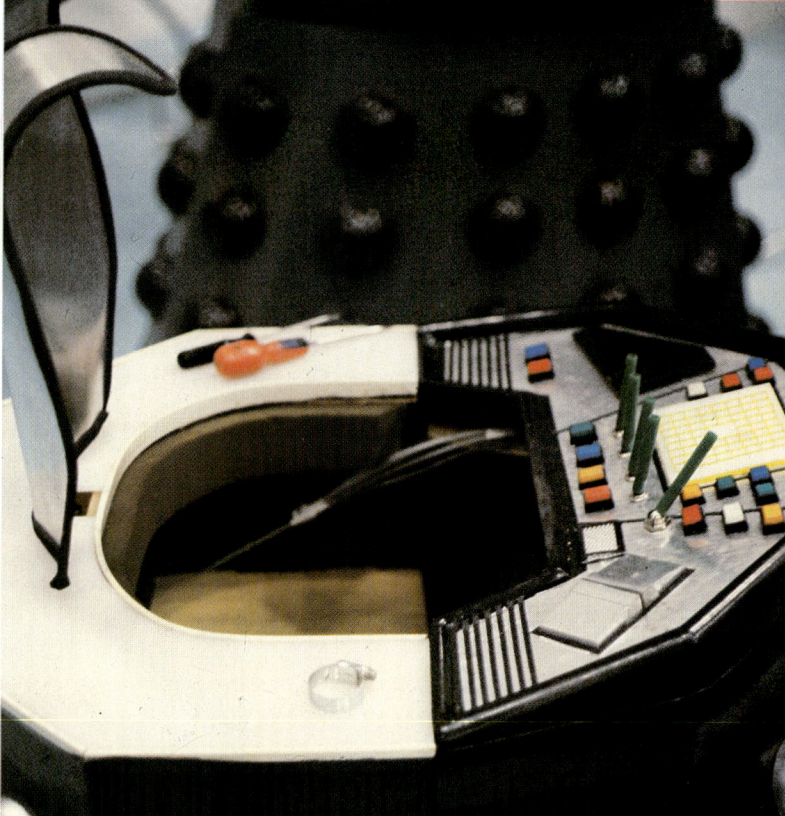

DALEK · DRAWING Nº 2
GENERAL DETAIL · MARK 4 MODEL.

SIDE ELEVATION

ABOVE **Daleks in the studio during 'Resurrection of the Daleks'. Most have actors inside but there is a Visual Effects version in the foreground.**

ABOVE LEFT **Early Dalek drawings by Jack Kine.**

BELOW FAR LEFT **Davros's control unit built on the base of one of the original Daleks.**

BELOW LEFT **The switches by which Davros supposedly controls his creatures. In reality, they work the lights.**

though introduced some new details of its own.

The Daleks, and Davros too, moved by collecting static electricity from the floor – or at least that is how the original story went. This detail was conveniently lost over the following years, but it did bring out an aspect of the Daleks' impracticalities. Daleks gliding across a relatively flat studio floor is one thing, but take them outside and it's something else! On a reasonable pavement, they were more or less fine, unless one of the operators got up a bit of a speed down a slope and then hit a bump. However, take them out into the countryside and how they ever took over the world is a mystery! Everywhere they went, boards had to be laid down to form the flat surface on which to roll. Wedges were carefully tapped into position under the boards to bring them up into line with one another, and the Daleks carefully rolled into position. Cameras were then positioned so that this non-authentic addition to the surroundings would not be seen, and the animated pepper-pots could continue their devastation without revealing their secret.

71

10
K-9 – THE DOG

THE ORIGINAL DRAFT of the script for K-9 by Bob Baker and Dave Martin stipulated that the character, Professor Marius, a dog lover, had created K-9 as companion, guard and computer, in the shape of a dog. The first Visual Effects Designer to read this was Ian Scoones as he was already working on the story concerned – 'The Invisible Enemy'. Unlike the majority of *Doctor Who* stories, there was no location filming, instead a great deal of effort was going into the model filming. Ian quickly realized that one Effects Designer could not really cope with all the work, and so a second Designer was brought in. Ian had done a certain amount of design work for this unusual 'special prop', but it was the new designer, Tony Harding, who came up with the shape that became K-9.

Like most *Doctor Who*s, there really was not enough time to design and build all the effects to our complete satisfaction, and the additional problem with K-9 was that he required radio-control which was a new venture for the Effects Department. Tony Harding had considered making this new creature big enough for a small person to hide in (like R2-D2 who appeared a few years later) but this idea was rejected as it was thought that it would be very obvious that there was an operator inside. So K-9 was made smaller rather than larger.

Radio-control itself is not all that new, but like any electronic device, it has benefited enormously over the last few years from the arrival of modern lightweight circuits. The design and construction of K-9 coincided with the end of the original style radio-control, and inherited many of its problems. Tony Harding reckons that he had about three weeks to have K-9 built, and at the same time he was of course working on all the other effects that had to be made for the story.

Baker and Martin's script did indicate what K-9 was expected to do, and from this the number of radio-control

RIGHT **K-9 in Hampton Court maze on one of his many adventures. Here he was helping out the presenters of 'The Computer Programme' and of course he discovered the quickest way out!**

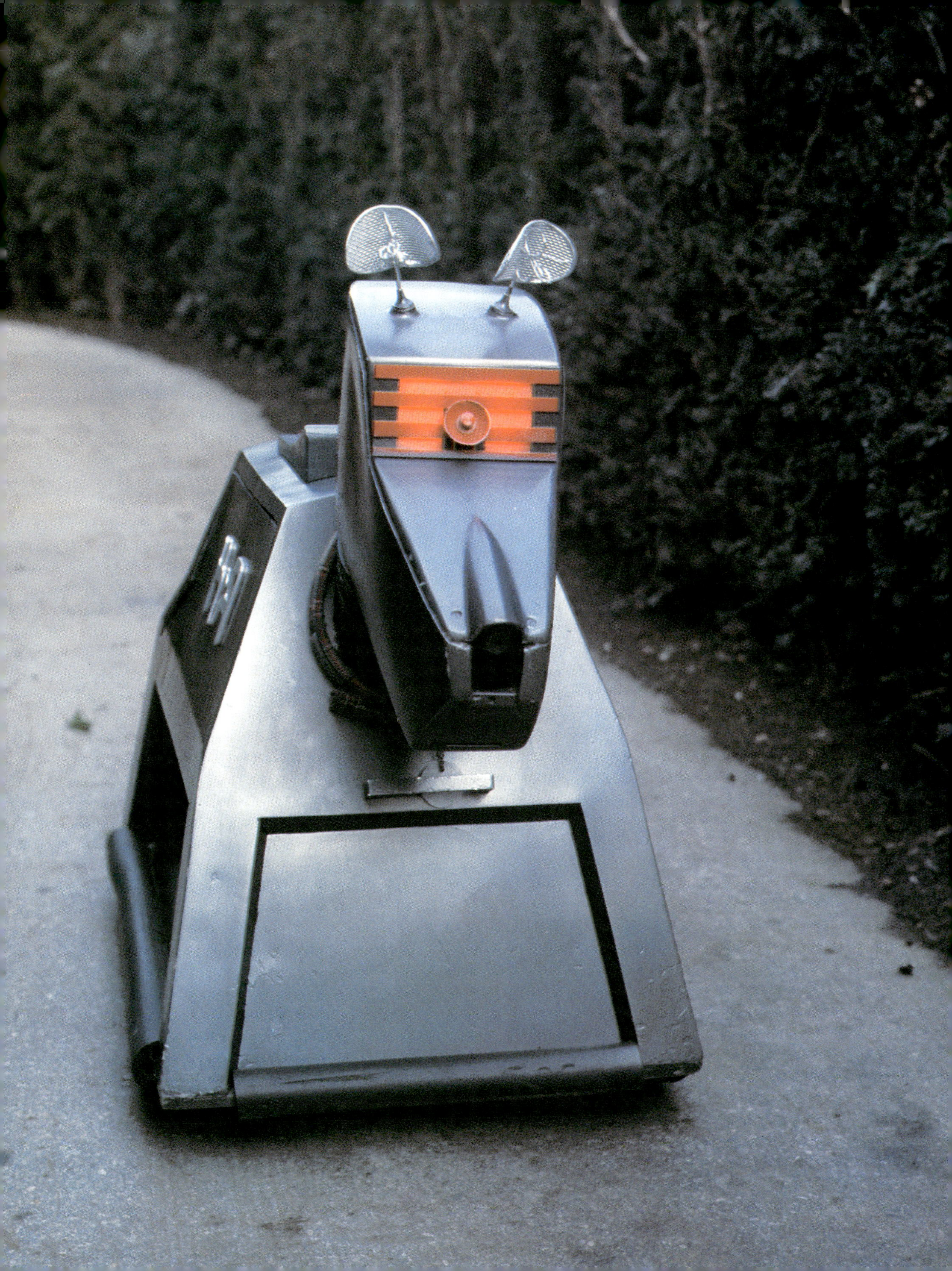

channels could be calculated. Ian Scoones had already bought the necessary radio-control gear: four- and six-channel Futaba sets which worked on the older AM frequency. This gave ten channels in total which was enough to run K-9 forward and back, steer him, wag his tail up and down and side to side, and provide six other functions. The first ran the computer panel on his back, which worked in conjunction with his eyes; the second operated his probe; the third, his ears and a fourth his nose gun. This left two channels which switched on a blue screen side panel, and a ticker-tape read-out from his mouth.

Tony's design for K-9 left a fair amount of room inside to fit all the necessary motors, batteries and switches. A windscreen wiper motor powered by small motorcycle-type wet-cell batteries drove a chain through to the rear axle. Switches for the other functions were constructed using standard model-aircraft-type servos operating micro-switches. However, although there was a fair amount of room inside, once the equipment was installed it was very difficult to get at if anything went wrong. K-9's body would lift off the chassis, but only after everything was disconnected, so you only resorted to this in cases of extreme emergency! K-9, thanks to hard work from many members of the Effects Department, was completed in time for the first studio. But then the major problem that stayed with K-9 for a very long time reared its head – interference!

Once in the studio it was found that not only did K-9's radio control interfere with the TV cameras, but the TV cameras interfered with K-9! The first few studio recordings were fraught with difficulty as K-9 had to be kept as far away as possible from anything electrical – which in a television studio is rather difficult. If K-9 or his controllers went anywhere near a camera, the radio signals would invariably cause patterns on that camera's pictures. Also some of the signals the camera itself generated would send K-9 into an electronic frenzy and steer him crashing into the nearest piece of scenery.

All in all, the first studio recordings with this new companion to the Doctor were not completely successful and it is a wonder that K-9 was kept in the stories. That of course was another problem that faced Tony Harding, no one knew if K-9 would just feature in 'The Invisible Enemy', or would stay with the Doctor as his most unusual companion to date. With hindsight, knowing that K-9 did of course stay for several seasons, Tony Harding reckons he would have approached K-9's design and construction somewhat differently, but at the time it seemed that K-9 was just a one-off special effects prop – even if he was a somewhat complicated one – and overall, Tony could not justify spending too much time and money on one story.

Once it was decided that K-9 was to stay with the Doctor, something had to be done about the teething troubles that had beset the first recordings. Besides the interference, there was also the problem that K-9 tended to get jammed when it climbed over the cables of the cameras, lights and the multitude of other electrical apparatus lying around the studio. Scenery could also pose a problem, for scenery doors always have a metal strap across the bottom, to help keep the door frame stable, and the original K-9 even had a problem coping with this thin bit of metal.

The first change that was made to K-9's mechanics was to modify him from being rear-wheel to front-wheel drive. This solved, to a certain extent, the problem with the scenery doors and with some types of cable, though admittedly only the very thin ones – K-9 would still jam climbing the rest! However, the dog continued in this form for many stories, still causing and receiving interference, though newer cameras in some of the studios solved some of the problems. K-9 has even been on location, which is something that Tony had never envisaged. But, with a dedicated stream of mechanics in the form of Visual Effects Assistants, plus a radio-control specialist, Nigel Brackley, on a full-time basis, the Dog (as he was tending to be called) continued in this Mark 2 form for several seasons.

K-9 was by now officially the Mark 2 version for, in the story 'The Invasion of Time', Mark 1 was presented to the departing Leela as a present. It was then decided to bring K-9 back into the series, and the only way this could be done was to have the Doctor build a new Mark 2 using data conveniently stored

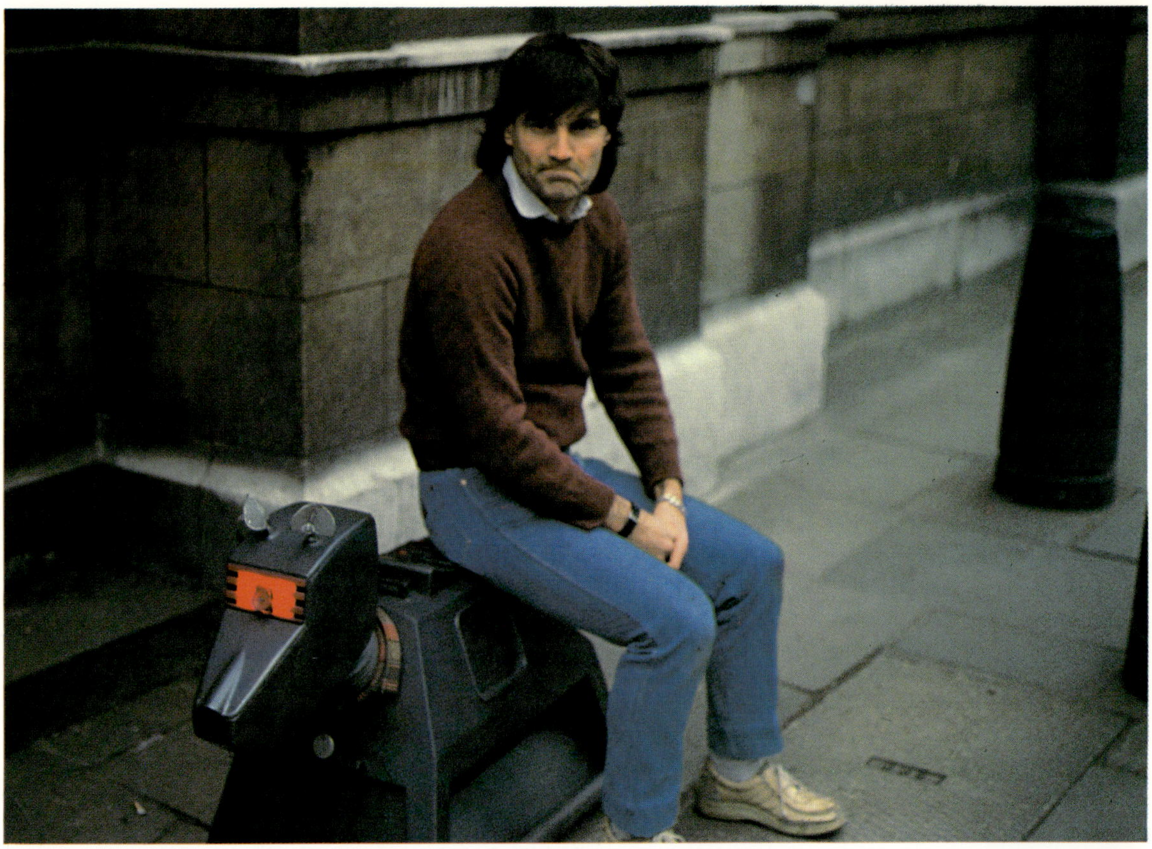

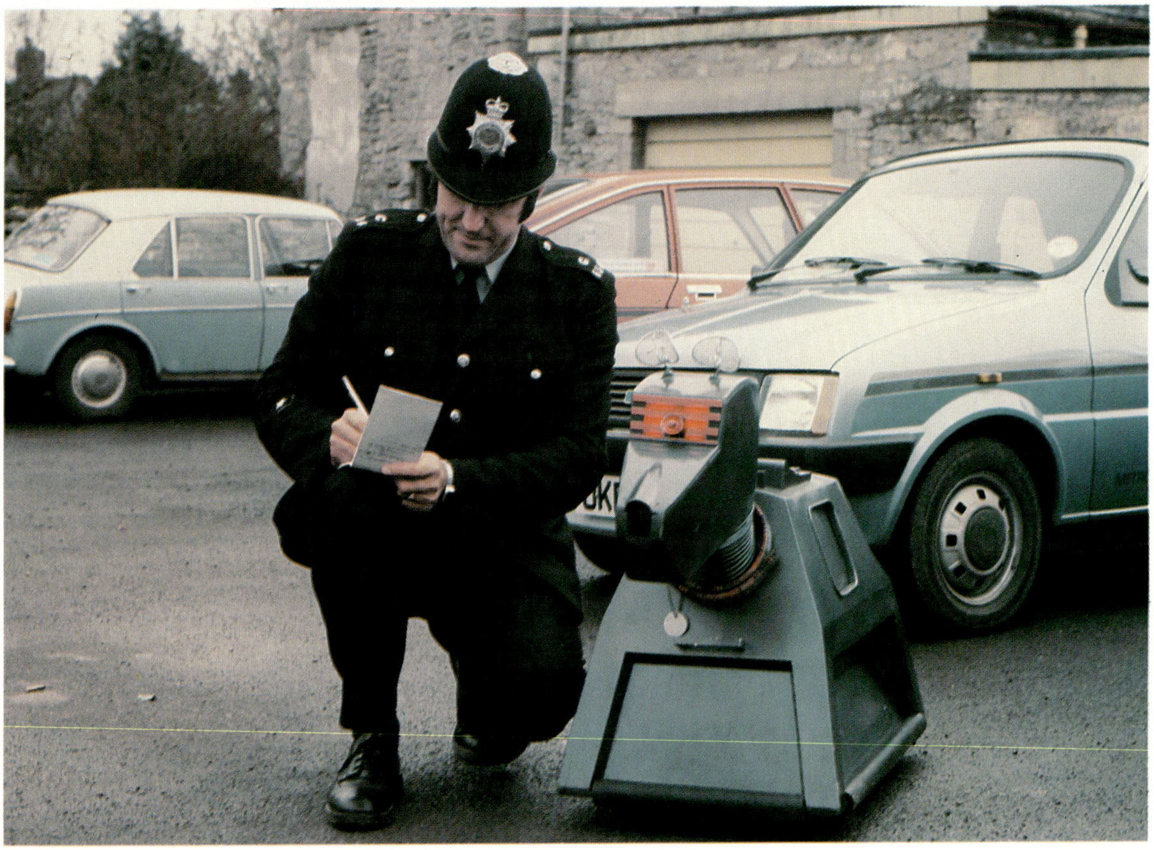

ABOVE LEFT **The author finding K-9 a rather uncomfortable seat outside the Science Museum during the filming of *Mat and Mutt*.**

BELOW LEFT **A break in the shooting of 'K-9 and Company' when the Dog met a friendly cop and narrowly avoided a parking ticket!**

within the Tardis. From an Effects point of view, the Mark 2 K-9 was the Mark 1 K-9 with a new coat of paint. The gold colour of the original gave way to a metallic charcoal.

Although I had worked with K-9, and had on odd occasions operated him when Nigel Brackley was unavailable, up to this point I had never really had anything to do with the design or modifications that had taken place over the years. But when the season that included 'Warriors' Gate' began (which of course starred the Dog) I was obviously concerned that he should be in good running order when we came to the recording. Tony Harding was working on another story, earlier than mine, and was even more worried! Eventually, I discussed the problem with one of my colleagues, Charlie Lumm, who specialized in many aspects of electro-mechanical effects work, and we jointly decided that there was nothing else for it, K-9 was going to have to be rebuilt, mechanically at least, and by now the troublesome radio control was also due for an overhaul.

I discussed this with Charlie one morning, then I went to lunch and by the time I came back, he had completely stripped out the insides of K-9, leaving an empty shell! Virtually all of the mechanics were rebuilt over the following two weeks. The front-wheel drive was retained, though with very much larger twenty centimetre diameter wheels, that meant at last K-9 could climb over cables and up shallow steps. A model racing-car differential was also fitted to the front axle, which allowed both front wheels to be driven. Originally it only had one-wheel drive, otherwise the wheels would have skidded on the floor every time K-9 was steered. Now with the differential, both wheels could be driven and K-9 would steer equally well in both directions. I had also decided at this point that it was an ideal time to update the radio control to the more modern FM type, which was much less prone to interference, and two six-channel MacGregor JR Series sets were bought.

The new improved K-9 was ready in time for Tony Harding's story, 'State of Decay', and for one of the studios I ran the Dog myself, as Nigel Brackley was unavailable. Everything went surprisingly well with the new mechanics and electronics, even though the steering was back to front and I kept driving him into the scenery! However, K-9 performed his first stunt by doing a flying leap out of the Tardis and managing not to turn on to his side in the process. By the time 'Warriors' Gate' came around later that year, all the new teething troubles had been cured and K-9 was working better than he had ever done. As I mentioned earlier, it was ironic that having got K-9 working so well, this story marked his last appearance in his Mark 2 guise, and he left at the end of the last episode with Romana.

Even if K-9 was not to feature in *Doctor Who* again, apart from his brief guest appearance in 'The Five Doctors', he has never been off the screen for long. He has guested on programmes as diverse as *The Computer Programme* and *The Generation Game*, visited conventions and opened several functions. He reappeared in his own story *K-9 and Company*, with Sarah Jane Smith, in his Mark 3 guise. This meant a new metallic blue paint finish, plus the addition of a couple of handles.

BELOW **On location during 'K-9 and Company'. The Mark 3 K-9 could travel over fairly rough ground but this sloping field was too much for him and he had to be manhandled into position.**

ABOVE **K-9's insides. The white drive batteries are just behind the black speed controller which hides the main motor. The radio control receivers are the black boxes at the centre top.**

Recently, I had the honour of appearing with him myself in London, ostensibly for me to do some research at the Science Museum. But it turned out more like a guided tour by K-9 as he insisted on telling me about every exhibit we passed.

One thing people often do not realize is that K-9's 'voice' has never come from inside his body. For television this is not important as the viewer cannot tell where the sound comes from. However, outside the television studios, it is a problem that has never been solved satisfactorily. John Leeson has always been 'the voice' of K-9 (apart from one season with David Brierly) and originally several electronic circuits were used to modify his voice into the Dog's. Now he can do the voice completely by himself, which does come in useful if he is on tour with K-9.

Lastly, everyone, but everyone, is intrigued by K-9's dog tag. They can only ever see a blank side so they always turn it round to see what is written on the other side. Unfortunately, that side is blank too; there has never been 'K-9' on it, and I suppose it is too late to change it now.

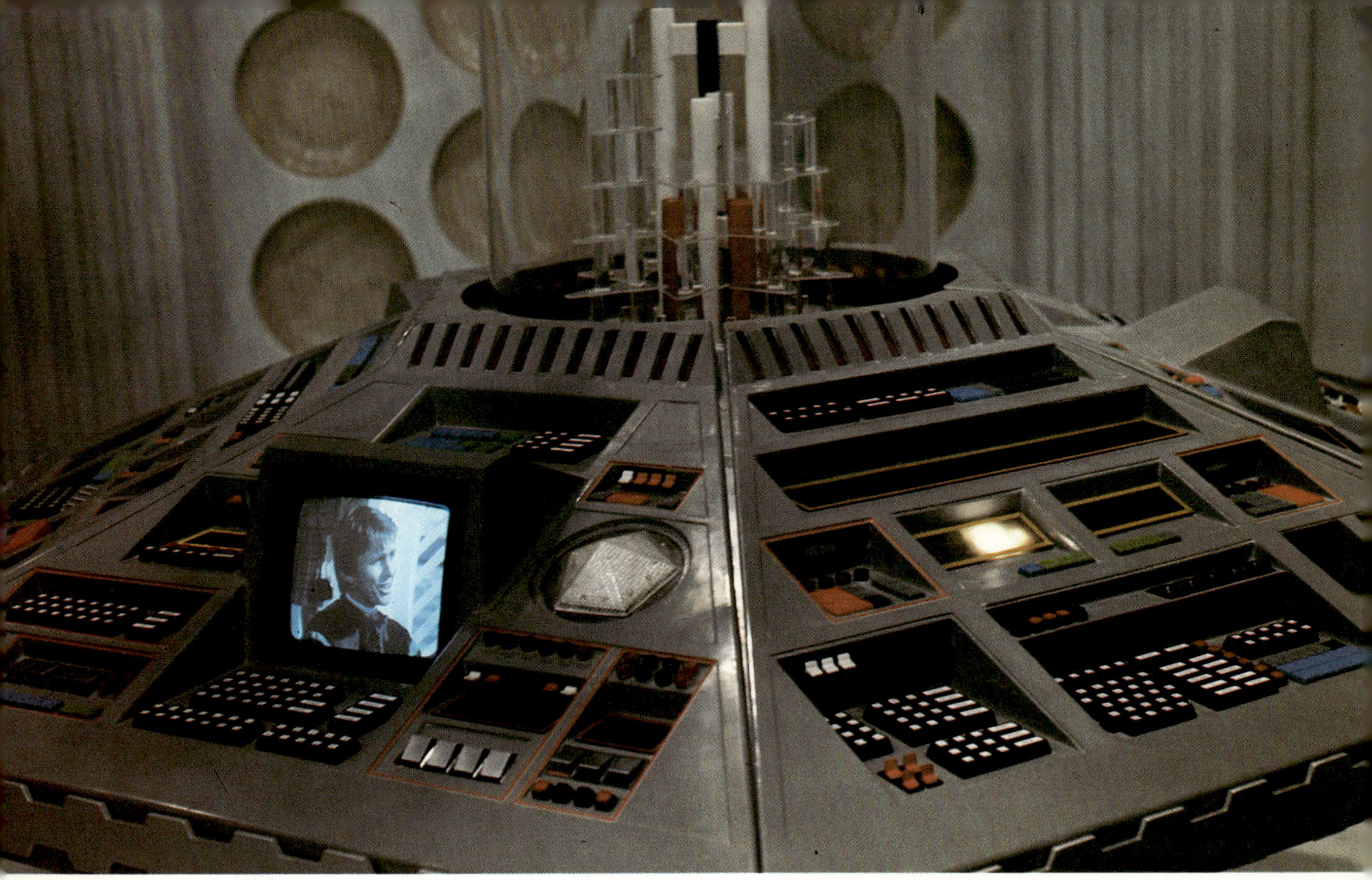

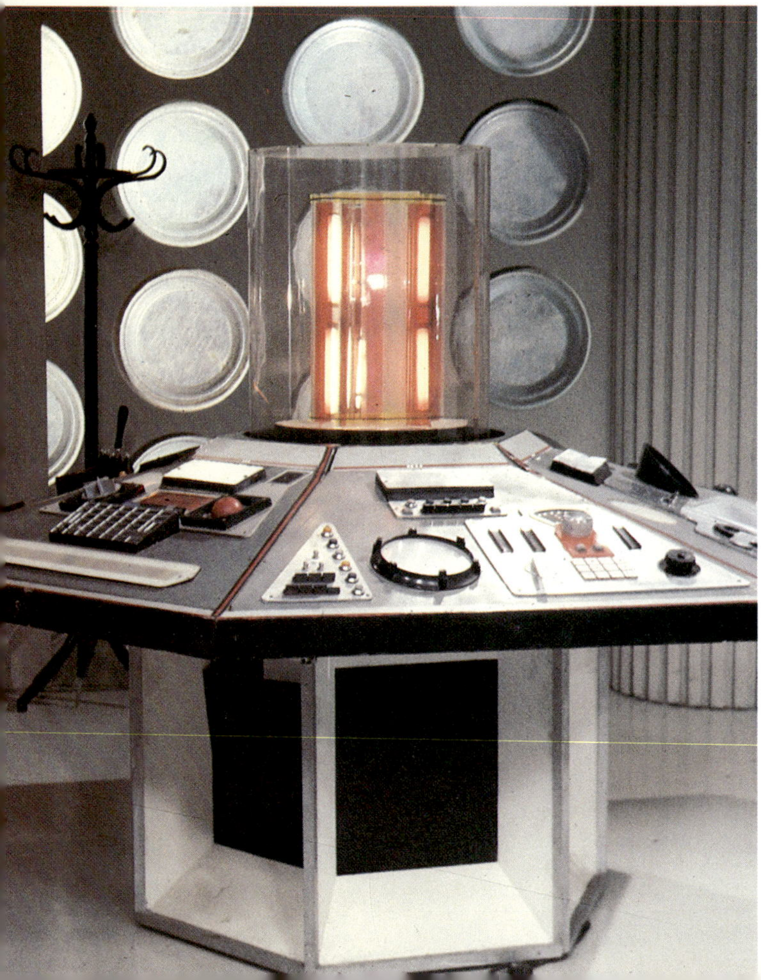

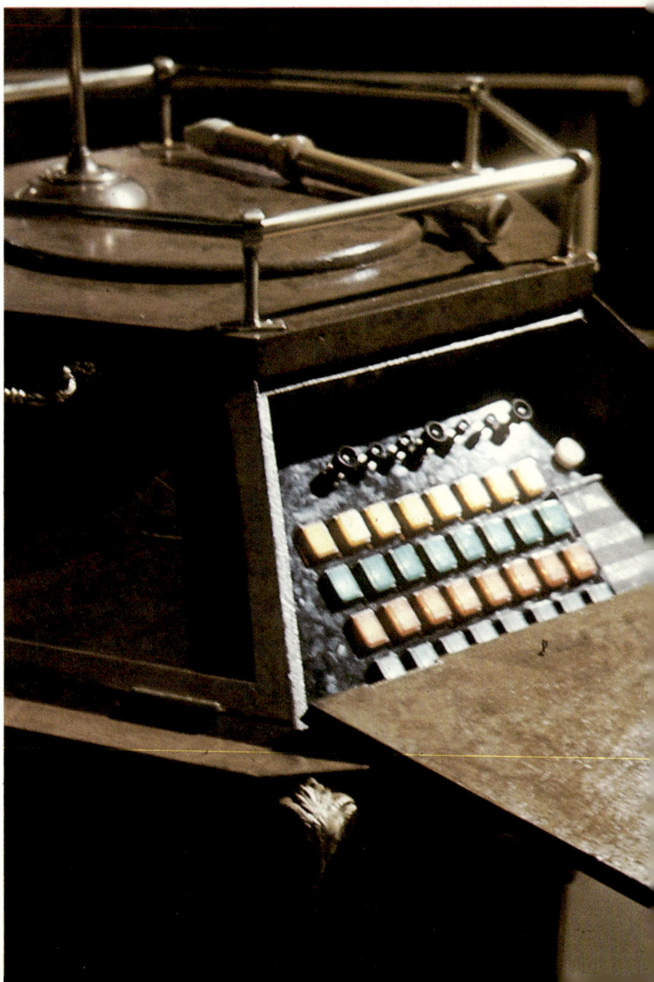

11
THE TARDIS

ARRIVING WITH THE Doctor in the very first *Doctor Who* episode came a craft that has to be considered as the weirdest spaceship ever devised. When the Tardis materialized in London, it needed to disguise itself as an everyday object, and, as it was 1963, it chose a police box. Like a telephone box, these stood on many street corners and allowed the policeman on his beat to contact the police station. The light on top would flash if the station wanted to call him. This was, of course, the days before the pocket radio. No one foresaw that twenty years later, the police box would be virtually unknown on the streets. The Tardis, however, has stubbornly remained in its original form and to most people now a police box *is* a Tardis.

ABOVE LEFT **The current Tardis console designed by Mike Kelt. The hexagon shape was retained but subtly updated using modern micro-circuitry and TV monitors. It is made of fibreglass and aluminium rather than wood.**

BELOW FAR LEFT **The original Tardis console which was forever being modified until eventually the panels and controls had to be replaced. It was made of painted wood.**

BELOW LEFT **The Edwardian-style console which replaced the original larger one. The control panels were hidden away under fold-down lids.**

The 'real' Tardis has an interior and an exterior but we have been unable to squeeze all the interior into the police box, so it has to remain as a separate set in the television studio. As far as the exterior disguise is concerned, the Tardis comes in several sizes for the making of a *Doctor Who* episode. There is the full-sized one used when people have to walk inside, and many model versions. The smallest model Tardis ever was just over one centimetre high. Of the other models, quite a few have been about one metre high (half the full-sized version) though the usual size for model filming is about fifteen centimetres.

My first connection with a *Doctor Who* story was when I had to adapt one of the miniature Tardis in order to make the famous lamp flash. This was for 'The Curse of Peladon'. The method by which the lamp flashed has roughly followed the progress of electronics over the years. The first attempts used a flasher bulb, which flashed at more or less its own rate and took a long time to get warmed up in the first place. Early attempts at miniaturizing circuitry came with an encapsulated electronic device meant to be an electronic metronome, but which in true effects fashion I adapted to a different, far more interesting purpose. This device would, without too much modification, flash a small bulb, and this provided the model Tardis lamp for many years. More recently, it was replaced with proper microcircuitry, which kept the lamp flashing regularly using very little current. In addition, the new electronics do not blow the bulb too often, a common problem with the older method.

If the exterior of the Tardis caused a few problems, that was nothing compared with those of the interior. Visual Effects' involvement has always revolved around the console, in its various forms, and the associated mechanics and electronics. The original console was constructed mostly from wood and survived until relatively recently. The main problem with this version was that it would only fit together one way, and given that it was a hexagon you sometimes had to try all six options before the hexagonal top fitted into the hexagonal centre. Six panels fitted into the six positions, with a variety of knobs, dials and switches on each. None initially was meant to do anything in particular, even the large lever with the big red knob that eventually ended up as the door opener! Originally, it was just a large lever with a big red knob. Other instruments were built in at the whim of various directors, and were then modified into something else. All the lamps were powered from packs of six-volt batteries and at the start of every new season you could bet that someone had forgotten to remove the old ones, and they would be corroded into their boxes. A more up-to-date approach to a power source did not come until very recently.

The Time Rotor in the centre did not fare much better over the years. This was powered by a large electrical motor which turned a cam attached to a connecting rod, in turn attached to the base of the Time Rotor. This was quite heavy and so put quite a lot of strain on the motor and mechanics. Besides making a noise it gradually, over the seasons, got more and more worn and the Effects team were forever servicing it in an attempt to keep it going. If it was going to break down completely, it would inevitably be in the middle of a recording: on one occasion during the recording of 'The Stones of Blood', three of us had to crouch down under the Tardis with a length of rope and work the Time Rotor by hand for a whole sequence. It was fairly strenuous work!

For the season beginning with 'The Mask of Mandragadora', it was decided that the Doctor would discover a second Tardis control room, and use that one instead.

The alternative control room was somewhat different from the original, with a different console. There was a definite Edwardian feel to the whole surroundings, echoed by the much smaller console. The console still retained the six sides but the panels were far more discreet, each being hidden away under a flap. However, the usual lamps and switches prevailed, though there was a slightly more logical layout to them. The years had taught us something! But this version did not last, and after the season the Doctor decided to go back to the other control room and the old console was unpacked yet again.

But the years were taking their toll. Having been blown up so many times, or having had bits removed and replaced upside down, the whole structure of the original console was nearing the end of its life. Eventually, the Producer, John Nathan-Turner, was persuaded by Effects Designer Mike Kelt to have everything redesigned and rebuilt.

Mike did not abandon the original concept, as had happened with the Edwardian version. Instead, he subtly updated the hexagon shape from aluminium and fibreglass, with TV monitors built in. The Time Rotor mechanism which had been rebuilt for the old console was transferred with a new Time Rotor structure on top. A vast new array of switches and lights were fitted to the new panels, many of which have still never been completely wired. The large lever with the big red knob was retained, in a slightly modified form, as the door opener, and was the only detailed feature from the original console.

Mains electricity, instead of batteries, now powers the lights, and feeds current to the monitors and Time Rotor lamps. Assembly is easier, as the hexagon will fit any way round, though it seems that only Mike Kelt knows exactly which panel goes where and only Charlie Lumm, who did the wiring, knows where all this attaches. But somebody else will untangle the mysteries and the Tardis will continue in its former glory.

12
'DOCTOR WHO' IN THE FUTURE

AT THE START of the *Doctor Who* saga, no one had any idea that over twenty years later the series would still be running, and be more popular than ever.

Doctor Who is now the longest running science fiction television serial in the world, and even if it ceased as of this minute, it would probably retain the record. The only other programme that has come close is *Captain Video* in America. Even *Star Trek*, which ranks alongside *Doctor Who* in popularity, was only made over three years (1965–7) although the re-runs do make it seem as if it has been going for ever!

Can *Doctor Who* continue? Even with the recent break, the series is approaching the quarter of a century mark, and there is no real reason why it should not continue for as long again.

The key to this success is that *Doctor Who* is unique. No other series can repeatedly change its lead star and still survive, especially where the lead *is* the series. In *Star Trek* for instance, although it might just be possible to change some of the actors and actresses, it would be extremely difficult to replace William Shatner as Captain Kirk or Leonard Nimoy as Mr Spock, without losing some of the faithful audience. But with *Doctor Who* it was written into the storyline very early on that Time Lords have to regenerate every so often, and that they need not necessarily regenerate into an identical character. Consequently, there should not be any problem about continuing the stories if the actor playing *Doctor Who* is changed. What *is* a problem, is the maintenance of the standards of production.

Television is constantly compared to the cinema. Those who work in television think that this is unfair comparison, but the

RIGHT **'Blake's 7' used many of the techniques developed by the BBC Visual Effects Department for** *Doctor Who*. **Here, for example, the computer ORAC on the far left and the teleport controls, centre right.**

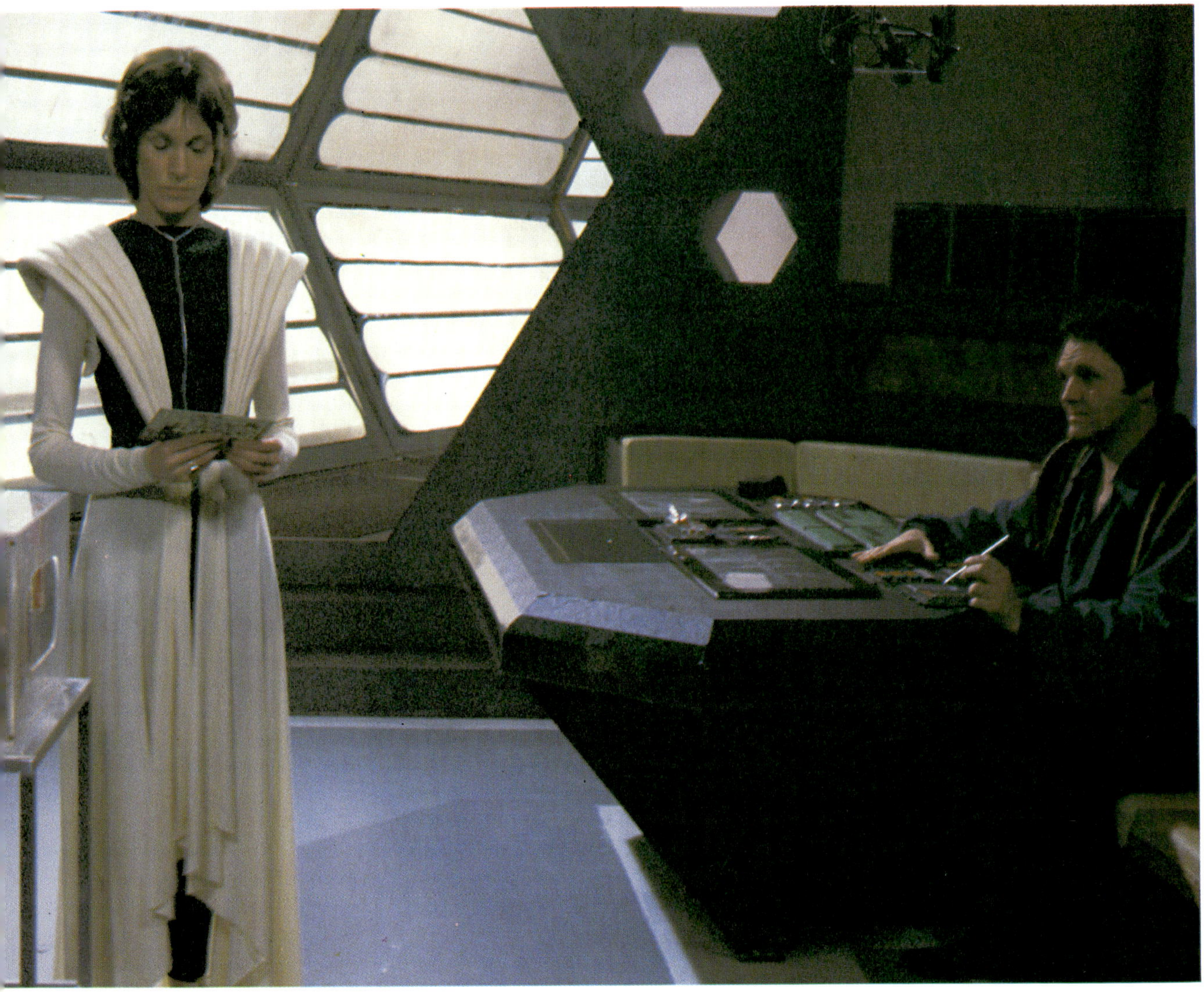

viewing public only see the final results on a screen, and no matter if this is a television screen at home, or a large film screen in a cinema, they will quite naturally make comparisons.

But a cinema film is made in a completely different way to a television programme, and especially to a BBC series like *Doctor Who*. Far more money is available to make a feature film and, what is possibly even more important, far more time. As I said very early on, a *Doctor Who* takes about three months to make, but feature films will normally take a year or so, and will

ABOVE **This is Quantel's Paintbox – a complete electronic painting system that allows the artist to paint as he would normally but using an electronic stylus and palette. The results are displayed in front of him on a TV screen.**

86

have far more people actually working on the production. Although the final length of a *Doctor Who* story, with its four half-hour episodes, is the same as a two-hour feature film, this is their only real connection. So for a *Doctor Who* we have to produce the same length of screen-time in a quarter of the time, with far less money.

But *Doctor Who* does have the advantage of being made on video, which is a far faster method than film, although these days even some cinema 'films' are being made using video, making them quick to make too, but that's another story.

The electronics of television can also speed up the production of *Doctor Who*, and this is one key area for development in the future. The host of electronic tricks, or 'electronic effects' give television a great advantage over film, for although everything done on video can also be done on film in some form or another, video is very much faster. The electronic effects such as Chromakey and CSO have already been mentioned, and to these can be added such tricks as making the picture turn around, flip over, act like the pages of a book, and even create a fairly reasonable 'explosion'. As a Visual Effects Designer, I still maintain I can do a better one 'for real', but I have to admit that the electronic version is not too bad. The growth of these electronic tricks has been made possible by the similar expansion in computers, for the computer memory is needed to store the vast amount of information that goes to make up even a single frame of television picture.

Computers though are also used in the film industry, particularly to control camera movements for model sequences. These are called Motion Control systems, and the same technique can be applied to a television camera. So, although the film and television industries are separate in many ways, a great number of new techniques can be equally applied to both.

The electronics are primarily there to speed up the time taken to make a programme, and given that using film takes longer than using video, they will probably make an even greater impact on feature films than on television. Computer-generated pictures are now being used to create sequences that only exist in the computer memory. Feature films like *TRON* and *The Last Starfighter* use computer-generated graphics extensively, and even films that are mostly 'film' have used electronics in particular sequences. One very good example of this is *Altered States* – the last two minutes or so was entirely computer-generated based on the original film picture.

Doctor Who, like all television programmes, has been able to take advantage of new electronic developments as they have come on to the market, along with some that are built by the BBC itself. This has meant that some tricks borrowed from the film industry have been able to be reproduced on television in a far simpler way. A good example is the transporter in *Star Trek*, compared with that in *Blake's 7* called a Teleport. They worked in a similar way, but the Blake method was far quicker because it used video.

Star Trek was made on film and the process to make the transporter 'work' was very complicated. If the crew had to be

BELOW **Here you can see a model tripod set against a CSO backcloth from 'The Tripods'. Since the whole series was made on videotape, electronic effects were widely used.**

beamed down from the ship to the planet, they first had to stand on the transporter pads. Then the transporter pads had to be filmed without the crew. Then a matte or mask had to be made of the crew. The shimmering effect that fills in their shape also had to be constructed and filmed and then all these bits of film had to be carefully put together in the right sequence. Even in its simplest form this took many days. However, aboard the Liberator things happened far quicker. *Blake's 7* was made on videotape (although many location scenes and model shots were filmed but then transferred to videotape). To 'teleport' Blake and his crew down to the surface all that was needed was one of those blue CSO backings. The crew were then 'overlayed' into the teleport and when they needed to disappear, were simply mixed out on the control desk. The shimmering effect was added at the same time by using electronic 'noise'. In all, if you were lucky, this effect took about five minutes to set up and record. Sometimes you were not so lucky and it took longer than five minutes, but even so it was still considerably quicker than shooting on film!

This very simple example shows why *Doctor Who* can be made as quickly as it can, and also why such series as *The Tripods* were made completely on videotape – even the location and model scenes.

Eventually, we should have High Definition television, which should give an even clearer picture. At present the number of lines that make up your television picture is 625. If you look very closely you can see them, and you can even count them if you cannot think of anything better to do! You will not actually count 625 as some are used to control the TV signal and for Ceefax and Oracle you use yet more lines. Present experiments are using 1200 lines, although there have been proposals for 2000 and more. All this means that you will see greater detail on your screen, and also that the screen can be made larger, without losing detail. At present if you expand a TV picture on a video projector you can easily count the lines without having to strain your eyes. High Definition will greatly help here. It will also mean that the more detail the viewer sees, the more detail will have to go into the set, costume or model.

In the future, when the scientists and engineers have perfected flat televisions, no thicker than pictures, which can hang on your wall, you will be able to have a television screen that occupies the whole wall. It will work in a similar way to the liquid crystal displays in watches and calculators. Although they may be a bit overpowering in the home, they will be very useful for exhibitions and conferences. Sony in Japan built a 'JumboTRON' television screen for the Japanese Expo exhibition in 1985 which can be viewed over a mile away. The technology that went into this will enable TV set manufacturers to build sets of all sizes that still give good pictures.

Apart from High Definition, there is also three-dimensional television using holography. A hologram is a three-dimensional photograph and is being used more and more on record covers, book covers and for pictures to hang on the wall. Moving holograms are also possible, and with a great deal of research, a Hologram Television set is not all that impractical. Do not go down to your local electrical shop and order one just yet!

So how will this affect *Doctor Who*, and those of us who make the programme? Any changes to the overall TV formats will probably have to come about gradually. High Definition will mean changing all the cameras, control desks, video machines and everything. And 3-D Hologram TV – should it ever arrive – will mean changing it all over again! So I think I can safely predict that we will continue in much the same way over the next few years at least. We will attempt to use all the newest techniques when it comes to designing and making effects. So we will be using new lightweight materials: microchip circuitry to flash the lights; and possibly even lasers to create new images. But these modern techniques do not replace the old ones completely. Just because some wonderful new way of doing a particular effect has been invented it does not automatically mean that the method we have been using for years will be abandoned for ever.

My favourite example of how modern technology sometimes lets us down concerns K-9. As I have revealed, K-9 is a mechanical beast, with radio-control, motors and gears. Some-

RIGHT **The latest in film technology is the Imax system. Using very large film, it projects an incredibly clear picture on to a giant screen. This film being shown at the National Museum of Photography, Film and Television, Bradford was shot by the space shuttle Challenger with an Imax camera.**

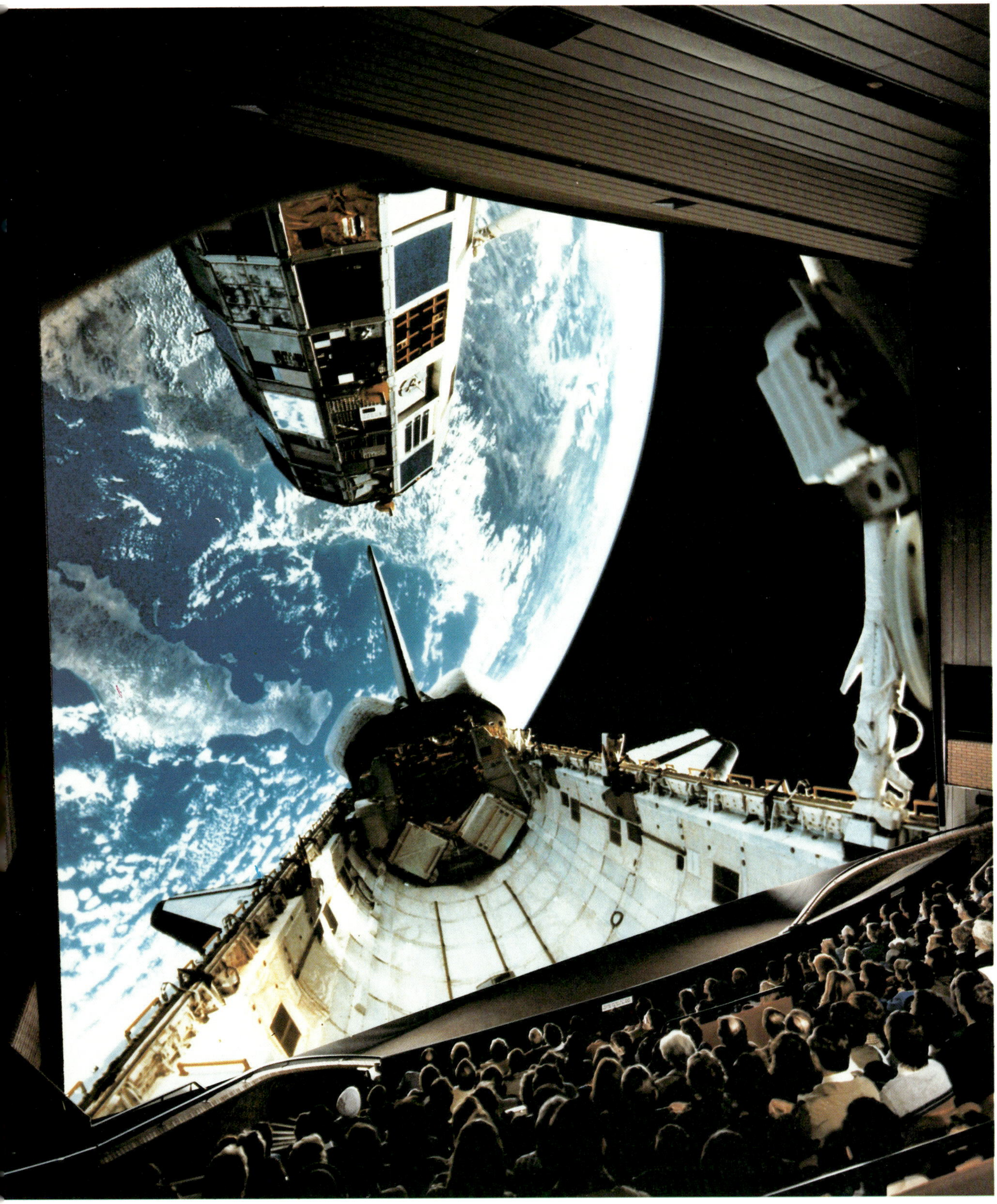

times this lot does not work exactly as planned. K-9's last appearance in a *Doctor Who*-related story was as the Mark 3 in 'K-9 and Company'. For his most triumphal rescue to date, he had to hurtle up a tree-lined path in a churchyard to attack a coven of witches around their fire. So that he could perform this task satisfactorily I had cleared the path, made sure that there were no odd stones or tree roots that could stop him, and that he had a clear run. It was the last shot on the day of location filming, and it was at night. K-9 was set into position, I hid with the radio-control transmitters behind a tree, the camera was started, and 'Action' was shouted. K-9 started very well, reached his top speed of about 5 m.p.h. and then ground to a halt. Tony Auger and I tipped K-9 over only to discover that the drive to his wheels had been destroyed and there was no way it could be repaired. But K-9 did make that final run, and faster than had been planned. Even with all the mechanics under his fibreglass shell, K-9 made that run through the churchyard and to the rescue pulled by Tony on fishing-line. So much for modern technology! It just shows that a fully-equipped Visual Effects box should always have at least one reel of fishing-line.

I wonder what the Doctor would have made of all this and I wonder if he can continue for ever? There is one sobering fact: the Time Lords can only regenerate twelve times, and if we assume that our first encounter with the Doctor was his first, he is already at number six. But even six more changes would mean he is around for some years to come, so there is not much cause for concern – yet!

CHRONOLOGY OF 'DOCTOR WHO' STORIES MENTIONED IN THIS BOOK

The Evil of the Daleks	1967
The Curse of Peladon	1972
Frontier in Space	1973
Planet of the Spiders	1973
Genesis of the Daleks	1975
The Pyramids of Mars	1975
The Mask of Mandragadora	1976
The Face of Evil	1977
Image of Fendahl	1977
The Robots of Death	1977
The Invisible Enemy	1977
The Stones of Blood	1978
The Invasion of Time	1978
City of Death	1979
The Leisure Hive	1980
Meglos	1980
State of Decay	1980
Warriors' Gate	1981
K-9 and Company	1981
The Five Doctors	1983
Warriors of the Deep	1983
Resurrection of the Daleks	1984
Vengeance on Varos	1985

GLOSSARY

COLOUR SEPARATION OVERLAY or CSO The method of combining two electronic images by using a background colour to switch or 'key' the second picture. The process is also known by the trade name of Chromakey, and the two processes work exactly the same.

FLOOR EFFECTS The overall name given to the majority of special effects that take place 'on the floor'. This can be in a studio or out on location.

HIGH SPEED FILMING By running a film camera faster than its normal speed of 24 or 25 frames per second, you effectively slow down the final scene. Used mostly for the filming of models and miniature explosions. For example if a miniature explosion is filmed at the normal speed, it will happen very fast, and it will not look realistic. If however it is filmed at, say, 100 frames per second, and then projected at the normal – for television – 25 fps, this will slow the explosion down as it will last four times as long.

MODELS AND MINIATURES The two terms tend to be used as meaning much the same, but although all miniatures are 'models', not all models are 'miniatures'. For example a large representation of an insect for a science programme would not be a miniature, though it is a model. For filming a programme like *Doctor Who* the models will all be smaller than they would be life size, i.e. 'miniatures'.

PROPS The usual shortened term for 'properties', which means any item used by the cast for a production. Everyday objects such as cups and saucers are props, and for *Doctor Who*, so are guns and radio communicators. However if the prop has to be made specially, or has to 'do' something, this invariably means that it becomes a 'special effects prop', made by Visual Effects. This usually applies to *Doctor Who* guns and radios.

PYROTECHNICS The term used for explosives in special effects.

STUDIOS and STAGES 'Studio' is the word used for the place where TV programmes are made using electronic cameras, such as the BBC Television Centre. However when film cameras are being used, these places are called 'stages'. But confusingly a group of film stages are collectively called 'studios', like Pinewood Film Studios or Ealing Film Studios.

STORYBOARD A series of pictures showing the main action of any story. Mostly these will be very quickly drawn sketches, but occasionally they will be very detailed and in colour.

TELECINE The machine that runs film for television programmes. It is a combination of a film projector and a television camera in the same case. It is usually referred to just by its initials, but this isn't as might be thought 'TC', but 'TK', so a Director will say 'Run TK', meaning start the telecine machine to run some film into the studio. (There are two possible explanations why 'TC' isn't used. As far as the BBC is concerned 'TC' is short for 'Television Centre', and in addition the 'cine' part of the name comes really from 'kine' with a hard 'k' sound.)

VT Really the shortened form of 'videotape'; the magnetic tape for recording pictures as well as sound. Usually the term is used for the videotape machine as well and so the Director will say 'Run VT', to start the videotape machine.

INDEX

Adric, 8
Airfix models, 47
Alien, 41
Altered States, 88

Baker, Tom, 18, 25, 35–6
Beam Machine, 25
Bentine, Michael, 8
Blake's 7, 26, 33, 85, 88, 89
Blue Screen Method, 53
Boris, 65–6
Buildings, model, 49–51, 56–9

Chromakey, 20, 87
'City of Death', 11
Colour Separation Overlay method, 20–3, 87, 88, 89
Communicators, 26–7, 34
Computers, 87–9
Costumes, 61–6
'Curse of Peladon, The', 81
Cybermats, 64
Cybermen, 62, 64

Daleks, 61, 67–71
Davros, 12, 69, 71
Draconians, 61

Effects, 9
Electronic effects, 86, 87 *see also* Colour Separation Overlay
Engineering Model Associates, 47–8
ET, 53
'Evil of the Daleks, The', 69
Explosions, 31, 34–5, 38, 46, 48–9, 52, 53, 54–5, 57–9, 87

'Face of Evil, The', 26, 43–4, 62, 64
Film, use of, 51–3, 56, 57–9, 88, 91
Fire *see* Pyrotechnics
'Five Doctors, The', 78

Flambeaux, 39
'Frontier in Space, The', 61

Galloping Galaxies, 22
'Genesis of the Daleks', 69
Gundan axe, 26, 29
Gundan robots, 18, 20, 29, 64

High Definition television, 90–91
Holography, 90
Hordas, 62, 64

'Image of the Fendahl', 12
Imax system, 91
'Invasion of Time, The', 75
'Invisible Enemy, The', 72, 75
It's a Square World, 8

K-9, 5, 12, 18, 19, 24, 28, 32, 40, 41–2, 64, 72–9, 90–2
  Mark 1 and Mark 2, 75–8
  Mark 3, 78, 92
'K-9 and Company', 12, 39, 77, 92

Marconiscope, 10
Martians, 6, 8
'Mask of Mandragadora, The', 83
Masks, 62–4
'Meglos', 17
Model kits, commercial, 46–8
MZ Laser Cannon, 24, 28, 34

Ogri, 38, 40–2
'100 Imperials' coin, 27, 29

Packard, crewman, 26
'Planet of the Spiders', 64–6
Privateer, 19, 20, 24, 26, 27, 28, 30, 32–3, 34, 35, 44–9, 53, 56–9
Professor, the, 25
'Pyramids of Mars, The', 10, 63
Pyrotechnics, 35–6, 49, 50, 53, 54–5, 57–9

Quantel Paintbox, 86
Quatermass, 7–8

Radio-control, 72–5, 77
'Resurrection of the Daleks', 69, 70
'Robots of Death, The', 64
Rollright Stones, 37, 38, 40
Romana, 24, 28, 30, 35, 78
Rorvik, 35

Sagan, crewman, 24, 35–6
Sea Devil, 34, 62
Silurians, 34, 36, 61, 62
Smith, Sarah Jane, 65, 78
Spaceships, 10–11, 19, 22, 33, 43–9, 52, 53 *see also* Privateer, Tardis
Spiders, 64–6
Star Trek, 84, 88–9
Star Wars, 53
'State of Decay', 12, 17, 45, 54–5, 77–8
'Stones of Blood, The', 8, 37, 38–42, 83

Storyboard, 53
Sutek, 63

Tardis, 9, 23, 26, 32, 33, 43, 49, 56, 80–3
Tharils, 20, 24, 28, 30, 35–6
Time Lords, 84, 92
Time Rotor, 82, 83
Tripods, The, 88

'Vengeance on Varos', 16
Videotape, use of, 51–3, 87, 89
Video Effects workshop, 21
Voyager, 22

Ward, Lalla, 35
'Warriors' Gate', 17, 18, 19–20, 23, 24, 27, 28, 29, 31, 32–3, 34, 35–6, 37, 44–51, 53, 56–9, 64, 77, 78
'Warriors of the Deep', 27, 34, 36, 56, 62
Weapons, 15, 24–6, 34
Woofers, 31, 34, 38